GLOBE FEARON
HISTORICAL CASE STUDIES

VOICES OF AMERICA

THE IMMIGRANT EXPERIENCE

GLOBE FEARON EDUCATIONAL PUBLISHER
Upper Saddle River, New Jersey
www.globefearon.com

CONSULTANTS

Nelson Acevedo is the Lead Assistant Principal for Social Studies at the Manhattan High School Superintendency. He has served as Social Studies Department Chairperson at Norman Thomas High School in New York City and Eastern District High School in Brooklyn, New York.

Patricia Allen Day is Associate Director of Secondary Social Studies for the Dayton, Ohio public schools. A teacher for 26 years, she has taught many different social studies classes. She is a William Jennings Scholar and was the recipient of the Excellence in Teaching Award from the Dayton Board of Education. She received her B.S. from Virginia Commonwealth University and her M.A. from Wright State University in Dayton, Ohio.

Martin Martin teaches at Edison High School in Fresno, California. For the last five years, he has taught math and Chicano/Latino history. He is the recipient of the Mellon Fellowship. He received his M.A. in Education from Stanford University.

Noreen Saunders is a teacher at South Miami High School in Miami, Florida. She received her B.A. from Rutgers University and her masters from Nova Southeastern University in Ft. Lauderdale, Florida. She teaches American history, world history, and advanced placement in U.S. history.

Virginia Yans is a professor of history at Rutgers, the State University of New Jersey. She has published several books and articles concerning the history of immigration and served for seven years as an advisor to the National Park Service and the Statue of Liberty-Ellis Island Foundation. She is the author of *Ellis Island and the Peopling of America: The Official Guide* and *Immigration Reconsidered: History, Sociology, and Politics.*

Executive Editor: Jean Liccione
Market Manager: Rhonda Anderson
Senior Editor: Karen Bernhaut
Project Editor: Lewis Parker
Writers: Gabriel Davis, Scott Ingram, Lewis Parker
Production Editor: Alan Dalgleish
Electronic Page Production: Mimi Raihl, Linda Bierniak, Phyllis Rosinsky
Photo Research: Martin A. Levick
Series and Cover Design: Joan Jacobus
Designer: Lisa Nuland

Printed in the United States of America 1 2 3 4 5 6 7 8 9 10 02 01 00 99 98

ISBN: 0-835-92313-4

GLOBE FEARON EDUCATIONAL PUBLISHER
Upper Saddle River, New Jersey
www.globefearon.com

CONTENTS

Soon after World War I, hundreds of thousands of immigrants came to the United States. This picture shows Bulgarians leaving for America.

OVERVIEW

THE AMERICAN MOSAIC

TERMS TO KNOW

- immigrant
- melting pot
- mosaic
- refuge

In the late 1800s, Israel Zangwill, a Jewish **immigrant**, arrived in the United States from England. An immigrant is a person who leaves one country to settle in another. In 1908, Zangwill's play "The Melting Pot" opened in Washington, D.C. In the play, he said, "America is the melting pot where all the races are fusing and reforming." The idea that the United States is a **melting pot** meant that once immigrants arrived here, they melted into the culture of the United States, losing the special cultures of their homeland in order to become Americans.

In the 1970s, President Jimmy Carter described the United States differently. He called the United States an "American Mosaic." In a **mosaic**, shapes of different colors are joined together to make a larger pattern. This notion differs from the idea of separate cultures being joined into one.

A more recent idea has to do with cultural balance. Today, many immigrants want to find a balance between the culture they brought to the United States and the culture they found here. They enjoy the culture of the United States, but they don't want to give up the best parts of their own culture.

To get an idea of how our country has been formed, look at a dollar bill. The American eagle on the back of the bill holds a banner with the words *E Pluribus Unum*—a Latin phrase meaning *From Many One.* The "many" are the millions upon millions of people who have come to America. Today, we understand that the richness of the United States is brought by immigrants and their descendants.

Except for those who can trace their ancestry back to Native Americans, most people in the United States are descended from immigrants. Even early Native Americans may have been immigrants, since they probably migrated to North America from Asia while following animals that they were hunting. They probably arrived in the Western Hemisphere 20,000 to 40,000 years ago.

From the 15th century through the establishment of the colonies, many groups of immigrants arrived in North America. Most of these immigrants came as explorers, colonists, and settlers. They sailed from ports in Spain, Portugal, England, Holland, Italy, and other European countries.

Within a short time, North America became a mix of many cultures. The Spanish conquered Native Americans in the south and southeast of what is now the United States. They set up the first permanent European settlement at St. Augustine, Florida, in 1565. The first permanent English settlement, founded at Jamestown, Virginia, was in 1607. The Dutch settled in the Hudson River valley; the Germans established footholds in the Pennsylvania area; the Portuguese came to the Massachusetts and New York areas; Swedes settled throughout the eastern seaboard, in areas of Delaware and New Jersey; the French settled along the St. Lawrence River; the Irish came to the New York and Boston areas. In the 1600s, Africans came as free people to Virginia. Less than a century later, the English, Spanish, Dutch, and others brought Africans against their will. These involuntary immigrants were enslaved and forced to work on sugar cane, tobacco, and cotton plantations. Until the 1840s, the number of Africans brought to North and South America as slaves was higher than the total number of all Europeans who migrated to the New World.

1 The Old Immigrants

From 1776, when the colonies declared their independence from Great Britain, to the early 1820s, not many immigrants came to the United States. During that time, only about 300,000 people emigrated—mostly from England. As the United States was expanding westward, land was available and many immigrants believed in the dream that they could make a new life for themselves.

Between 1820 and 1860, immigration greatly increased—more than eight million immigrants came to the United States. A few immigrants came from China; most came from countries in Northern and Western Europe. Immigrants arrived from England, Norway, France, Sweden, Germany, and Ireland. These immigrants helped to settle the American frontier, to energize the growing number of cities, and to begin building the transportation networks that linked the nation.

Immigrants came to the United States for several reasons—to escape from wars, to own land, to enjoy freedom of religion, to find jobs, and to seek adventure. Many Irish came because of a terrible famine. In the late 1840s, a plant disease destroyed the entire potato crop in Ireland causing widespread starvation. More than one million people died. Nearly two million came to the United States.

Thinking It Over

1. What were some of the reasons that immigrants came to the United States?
2. **Drawing Conclusions** How might coming to the United States have changed the lives of immigrants?

This picture shows Uncle Sam (the United States) offering ***refuge****, a safe place, for immigrants from countries throughout the world. The sign tells why many immigrants might want to come to the United States.*

2 The New Immigrants

From the 1880s through 1920, more than 23 million immigrants streamed into the United States. Immigrants continued to come from Northern and Western Europe, but beginning in the 1890s, most immigrants now came from Southern and Eastern Europe.

Seeking Opportunities

Most of the "old immigrants" had been Protestant, and they were people whose primary language was English. The "new immigrants" worshipped in many ways—they embraced Roman Catholicism, Eastern Orthodox Catholicism, and Judaism. They spoke many languages. In addition, many were unable to read and write.

Many of these people were Italians, Greeks, Jews, Poles, Rumanians, Austrians, Hungarians, and Russians. They left their homelands because of devastating wars, high unemployment, overpopulation, and epidemics of deadly diseases. The Jewish population of the United States increased from about 250,000 in 1877 to almost five million by 1927 as Jews fled from the massacre of their people in Russia.

The United States offered opportunities not available in Europe. The democratic system of government in the United States was attractive to many newcomers. Growing U.S. industries offered jobs to laborers who would work cheaply—many Italians went to work in coal mines; Portuguese, Greeks, and Italians went to work in textile mills; and Jews went to work in the garment factories.

Ellis Island

When the U.S. Constitution was adopted, it did not include restrictions on immigration. Until the 1880s, individual states decided which immigrants could enter the United States. With the passage of the Immigration Act of 1891, the federal government took control of immigration and, for the first time, restricted its flow. In order to make sure that immigrants were healthy, able to support themselves, and did not hold ideas that might be dangerous to the U.S. government, the nation passed this law creating immigration stations where immigrants would be detained and checked. The two major stations were located close to places where most immigrants arrived in the United States. The Ellis Island station, in New York Harbor, opened in 1891. The Angel Island station, near San Francisco, opened in 1910.

More than seven out of every ten immigrants who arrived from Europe came through the Ellis Island immigration station. At Ellis Island, immigrants were held while they were questioned and inspected before being allowed to start new lives in the United States. Between 1892 and 1954, more than 12 million immigrants passed through the waiting rooms, dormitories, and hospital wards of Ellis Island. In Case Study 1, you will find more information about immigrants' experiences at Ellis Island.

Chinese and the Land of Gold

When the United States acquired California in 1848, many companies sent advertisements to China that presented the United States as a golden land where Chinese immigrants would find high wages, large houses, and fine food. News of the discovery of gold caused thousands to come to California seeking their fortunes. By 1860, about two-thirds of all the Chinese in the United States worked in gold mines. When mining declined in the late 1860s, about 10,000 Chinese found work building the transcontinental railroad.

When the transcontinental railroad was completed, Chinese laborers took jobs in other industries throughout the West. Case Study 2 focuses on Chinese immigrant experiences in the United States.

Changes in Immigration Laws

Life was not easy for most immigrants. They usually settled in cities where they could find work. Because most immigrant neighborhoods were located in a city's poorer sections, immigrants often lived in crowded buildings with poor sanitation and safety.

Besides living in terrible housing conditions, many immigrants also faced prejudice from native-born Americans. Prejudice became extreme against immigrants arriving in the 1880s. Some Protestants, for example, feared the growing number of Catholics and Jews who were arriving from Southern and Eastern Europe. Some immigrants brought with them political beliefs that many Americans did not understand. Immigrants were also competing with native-born citizens for jobs that were becoming scarce.

Starting in the 1920s, the United States has adopted laws that restrict immigration. Case Study 3 tells about changes in immigration laws, the reasons for the changes, and the effects of immigration laws on the United States.

By the 1880s, giant steamships carried immigrants to the United States. This poster advertises an Italian steamship company. Between 1880 and 1924, about 4 million Italians emigrated to the United States. The poster states that this steamship also took immigrants to South America.

West Indian Immigrants

The effect of the Emergency Quota Act of 1921 was to decrease the number of immigrants from Southern and Eastern Europe. However, it did not restrict immigration from countries in the Americas. As a result, large numbers of immigrants from the West Indies in the Caribbean Sea came to the United

This photo shows an immigrant mother with her children as they arrive at the Ellis Island immigration station. Immigrants usually wore their best clothes to greet friends and relatives waiting for them.

States. Most of these immigrants traveled to New York City and lived in an area called Harlem.

About the same time that West Indian immigrants were pouring into Harlem, thousands of African American migrants from the South were arriving there too. In the 1920s, this unique combination of Southern African American migrants and West Indian immigrants helped to produce the Harlem Renaissance—a rebirth of artistic activity. Case Study 4 explains how West Indian newcomers enriched American culture.

Irish Political Power

Between 1820 and 1850, Irish immigrants made up 42 percent of all immigrants to the United States. Because large numbers of Irish came to the United States and because they were mainly Catholic, many native-born Americans saw them as a threat to the "American way of life." In order to make their lives better and fight against prejudice in the United States, the Irish turned to politics. Case Study 5 tells both about the Irish contributions to politics and about how their political organizations brought citizens into the political process who had never before felt a part of it.

Reforms in Working Conditions

Immigrants usually worked at the lowest-paying jobs—jobs that were dirty and dangerous. They often worked 11 or 12 hours a day and 6 days a week in such industries as textile factories, mines, or canneries.

In order to change working conditions throughout the United States, many immigrants joined unions and forced the adoption of laws that limited the number of hours people could work and that created safer workplaces. It was a long and hard struggle, but immigrants played a leading role in bringing about labor reforms for all workers. You will read more about how immigrants influenced labor reform in Case Study 6.

Community Organizations

In recent times, newcomers to the United States have developed various organizations to help others who come from their countries find jobs and housing. Cuban immigrants make up one group that has developed self-help organizations. More than 200,000 Cubans came to the United States in the 1960s after a revolution placed dictator Fidel Castro in charge of a Communist government in Cuba. In 1980, about 125,000 more Cubans fled Cuba.

Case Study 7 focuses on the Cuban American National Council (CNC), an organization based in the area of Miami known as Little Havana. The CNC helps Cuban immigrants find housing, employment, and community services. The CNC also encourages Cubans to continue their education and create businesses.

Thinking It Over

1. In what ways did immigrants try to improve their living and working conditions in the United States?
2. **Drawing Conclusions** How might immigrants' expectations of life in the United States been different from the reality they encountered?

3 Seeking the American Dream

Requests for citizenship are higher now than at any time in U.S. history. These requests increased from about 200,000 in 1991 to more than 1.5 million in 1997. For each of these immigrants, achieving the American Dream means something different. It may mean starting a business, practicing a profession, or owning a home—it may also mean having a steady job and food on the table. For some immigrants, it may mean that their children will get a better education than they received. For others, it may mean that they want to make a difference and improve life for all Americans.

In Case Study 8, you will find the stories of four immigrants who say they have achieved the American Dream. They all brought with them a determination to succeed in a land that offered them hope. Their success shows that the United States is as much a lure today for immigrants as it was for the newcomers of the 18th and 19th centuries. The accumulated experiences of all these immigrants are what has made and continues to make us a country.

In his 1998 State of the Union Address, President Bill Clinton spoke about the promise of the United States. He said,

> *Our cities are . . . still the gateways for new immigrants, from every continent, who come here to work for their own American dreams.*

Thinking It Over

1. **Drawing Conclusions** Why do you think different people have different definitions of the term "American Dream"?
2. **Forming Opinions** How would you describe the culture of the United States—melting pot, mosaic, or balanced? Explain your answer.

This painting, called "The Battery," shows immigrants arriving at the port of New York City in the 1850s. Castle Gardens, an immigration station which opened in 1855, is at the left in the painting.

The first sight of the United States that immigrants often saw was the Statue of Liberty welcoming them.

CASE STUDY 1

COMING TO AMERICA

CRITICAL QUESTIONS

- What did most immigrants experience during their journey to America?
- What challenges do people face when adjusting to life in a new country?

TERMS TO KNOW

- steamship
- Ellis Island
- steerage
- detained
- deported
- tenements

ACTIVE LEARNING

This case study focuses on what many immigrants experienced while traveling to America, passing through Ellis Island, and starting a new life in America. Some immigrants wrote letters home, describing these experiences. As you read this case study, think about what you might have seen and felt if you were an immigrant traveling to America. As you read, look for the Active Learning boxes. They will suggest ideas for you to use as you write your own letter.

Renee Sidler, an immigrant from Switzerland, boarded the Isle de France **steamship** with high hopes. Steamships were large steam-powered ships that carried passengers across the ocean. Renee's journey would bring her to the United States, where she dreamed of beginning a new life.

As far back as Renee could remember, she had wanted to see how other people lived. She had heard exciting stories about life in the United States. When an American family offered her a job as a nanny, she quickly accepted.

"I didn't know anyone else in the country, but I wanted to see America," she recalled. "The family offered to pay for half of my ticket."

As the ship began its two-week journey, Renee joined other passengers on the sunny deck. Most, like Renee, were immigrants on their way to a new life in a new land. During the first few days at sea, Renee and the others laughed, danced, and sang on the deck. Some evenings, Renee played music on her accordion. It seemed as if the trip would go smoothly.

Then, during the second week, a powerful storm struck. "People were screaming. Children were crying. The boat rode up and down, up and down, jumping waves," Renee recalled. "Many things crashed and broke. Many of us got seasick."

Swiss immigrant Renee Sidler (at right) said her biggest thrill of the trip was eating dinner at the captain's table.

Luckily, within two days the storm passed. Then both the ship and the passengers settled down again. A few days later, they approached land. In the distance, they could see the Statue of Liberty. Renee recalled,

> *We thought we had never seen anything so beautiful. Parents lifted their children to their shoulders. People waved to the statue as if it were alive. We knew it meant we had finally arrived in America.*

1 The Golden Door

Like Renee Sidler, immigrants over many years endured the hardships of leaving home and traveling in order to make new lives in the United States. They could enter the United States through several ports. Many Europeans came through Boston, Philadelphia, Baltimore, or ports along the Gulf of Mexico. Los Angeles, San Francisco, and Seattle became the entry points for many Asian newcomers. However, more than 70 percent of all immigrants came through New York City. This port came to be called the "Golden Door."

In the 1800s, immigrants coming to New York City entered at a port near the southern tip of Manhattan. Then, in 1892, the federal government opened an immigrant station on **Ellis Island** in New York Harbor. This immigration station was near where the Statue of Liberty had been erected in 1886.

Ellis Island was the result of a change in immigration policy that was adopted by the U.S. government. Before the 1880s, individual states selected those immigrants who were allowed to enter the United States. There were usually no restrictions on immigrants. However, by the late 1800s, attitudes were changing about how important the federal government was. Many people began to think that the federal government should improve people's living conditions. During this time, for example, laws were passed to control how many hours people worked, to make sure that food sold in stores was safe, and to create public parks.

As part of this new attitude, Congress passed the Immigration Act in 1891. This law aimed to

By the late 1930s, the Ellis Island immigration station consisted of 30 buildings, including the processing center, a dining room, and a hospital that had 125 beds.

keep immigrants at holding places to protect them from people who might take advantage of them. It also aimed to protect the nation from particular immigrants.

The Immigration Law created the Office of the Superintendent of Immigration. Its purpose was to set certain requirements that immigrants had to pass before coming into the United States. Ellis Island was opened as one of the places where immigrants could be detained until they were checked.

Traveling to America

Steamships offered three ways to travel—first, second, and third class. First-class passengers had the largest and most comfortable cabins. Second-class passengers traveled in smaller, less expensive cabins.

Most immigrants could not afford the price of first- or second-class tickets. They traveled in third class, or **steerage**, a large open area beneath the ship's deck. In the early 1900s, a steerage ticket cost $15 to $20, which would equal about $800 today.

On large ships, as many as 2,000 immigrants crowded into steerage. To get there, they climbed down dark, slippery stairways. The first thing they would have noticed was the thick, foul-smelling air. They soon came to a large room lined with hundreds of narrow bunks stacked one on top of the other. They would live in this area for the next two to three weeks.

Immigrants were assigned bunks. They had little space in which to store their belongings and barely enough room to sit up in bed. There was no place to shower and little privacy for washing or using the few toilets available. At mealtimes, immigrants waited in long lines for food that was served from 25-gallon tanks.

Most immigrants remember steerage as a difficult, unhealthy, and uncomfortable experience. An Italian immigrant recalls his journey in 1920 at age ten,

> *I remember the passage. It took us darn near a month to get here in the poorest type of accommodations; just like cattle in the hold of the ship, with no privacy, no nothing.*

A Good Movie to See

Ellis Island. The History Channel, 1997 (150 minutes)

Narrated by Mandy Patinkin, this three-cassette documentary presents an overview of the immigrant experience from 1892 to the 1940s. Immigrants of diverse backgrounds recall their adventures, from the passage across the sea to the challenge of starting a new life in America.

Everyone just huddled together. Animals, I think, travel better today than we did in those days coming across.

By the 1930s, many ocean liners had improved steerage conditions. They offered third-class cabins that slept up to six passengers, dining rooms, and more toilets and showers. However, older ships continued to operate with crowded, uncomfortable conditions.

Hope

As did many who traveled to the United States by sea, Renee Sidler felt seasick for most of the trip. But she knew things were even harder for immigrants traveling in steerage. Still, Renee recalls a feeling among the passengers of "we're all in this together." Her closest friend on the ship was a young, frightened steerage passenger named Marie. Renee and Marie spent time talking about their hopes and dreams for the future.

Passengers tried to remain optimistic and to look out for one another. As a Scottish immigrant recalled,

Our fellow voyagers were a mixture of every nationality in the world, all bound for a new life and happiness in the United States. For the most part they were all kindly people trying hard to help each other out and to make the best of a trying trip, even though they could not understand a word the other said.

Thinking It Over

1. Why did so many immigrants travel in steerage?
2. **Making Inferences** How might travel conditions have contributed to the spread of disease among steerage passengers?

Active Learning: Take notes about the conditions in steerage during the long overseas journey, about what it felt like to travel through a storm, and about how immigrants felt when they first saw the Statue of Liberty.

Large steamships could carry more than 2,000 immigrants in third class. Third class was called steerage because it was located where the steering mechanism of the ship was once placed. Steerage passengers took ferries from their steamship over to Ellis Island. There, they were examined by immigration officials.

2 Welcome to Ellis Island

Thousands of immigrants arrived daily in New York Harbor during the early 1900s. After a long, difficult journey they were tired and weary. Yet, at the first sighting of land, they jumped to their feet with a surge of excitement and a great feeling of relief. They had finally arrived!

The Statue of Liberty

One of the first sights immigrants saw as they approached the harbor was the Statue of Liberty. With her hand holding a beacon of light, she seemed to welcome them to America. One immigrant remembers,

> *The first time I saw the Statue of Liberty all the people were rushing to the side of the boat. "Look at her, look at her," and (in all kinds of languages) "There she is, there she is," like it was somebody who was greeting them.*

The Statue of Liberty was a gift from France to the United States in remembrance of how the two countries fought together during the American Revolution. Lady Liberty was given to the United States in 1886. Then, as now, she stood for freedom and independence. For millions of immigrants, she was that—and more. She was a towering symbol of the American Dream.

Ellis Island

Although immigrants rejoiced at their safe arrival in the United States, for most of them the journey was not yet over. Immigrants were questioned and inspected by doctors and other workers at Ellis Island. Only those immigrants who were healthy and who could support themselves would be allowed to enter the United States. Immigrants who did not pass inspection would be sent back to Europe. Between 1892 and 1954, more than 12 million immigrants passed through the waiting rooms, dormitories, and hospital wards of Ellis Island.

When the steamship stopped in New York Harbor, Renee said a quick good-bye to her friend Marie. They would never see each other again.

Doctors came aboard to inspect the first- and second-class passengers. Most of these people were immediately given permission to go. Renee passed inspection quickly. She collected her baggage and went to meet her new employers.

Meanwhile, Marie waited with the other steerage passengers. Before long, a ferryboat arrived to take them to Ellis Island. An English immigrant recalled the fear and confusion of that trip,

> *We were put on a barge, jammed in so tight that I couldn't turn 'round. There were so many of us, you see, and the stench was terrible. And when we got to Ellis Island, they put the gangplank down, and there was a man at the foot, and he was shouting, at the top of his voice, "Put your luggage here, drop your luggage here. Men this way. Women and children this way." Dad looked at us and said, "We'll meet you back here at this mound of luggage and hope we find it again and see you later."*

Most immigrants spent about five hours in the crowded Ellis Island inspection rooms. Tall iron railings separated the room into sections.

Thinking It Over

1. What did the Statue of Liberty represent for immigrants?
2. **Comparing** Once the ship arrived in New York Harbor, in what way were steerage passengers treated differently from other passengers?

3 Passing Inspection

Almost all immigrants spent about five hours at Ellis Island before entering the United States. Most passed a series of medical, mental, and legal inspections with little or no trouble.

Others did not pass so easily. They had to wait for more testing. As they waited, they became more and more worried. On the ship, they had heard stories of people being held at Ellis Island for many days. Some were even sent back across the ocean to their homeland.

Medical Inspection

The inspection process began with a quick medical check. Doctors from the U.S. Health Services inspected the immigrants' hair, mouth, skin, and eyes. In checking newcomers' eyes, doctors used a buttonhook, a metal tool used to button gloves. Doctors used it to pull back eyelids to check for eye diseases. They also checked for limps, breathing trouble, and heart problems.

If doctors found something wrong, they marked the immigrant's clothing with chalk—an "E" for eyes, an "H" for heart, and so on. Immigrants marked with chalk were given a more complete medical examination.

When an illness was confirmed, immigrants were sent to the Ellis Island hospital. They stayed there for a few days or weeks while they were treated. Once they recovered, they were released.

One immigrant remembered such an experience at Ellis Island,

> *We lived there for three days—Mother and we five children. My sister had been so ill and had cried so much that her eyes were absolutely bloodshot, and Mother was told, "Well, we can't let her in." But fortunately, Mother was an indomitable spirit and finally made them*

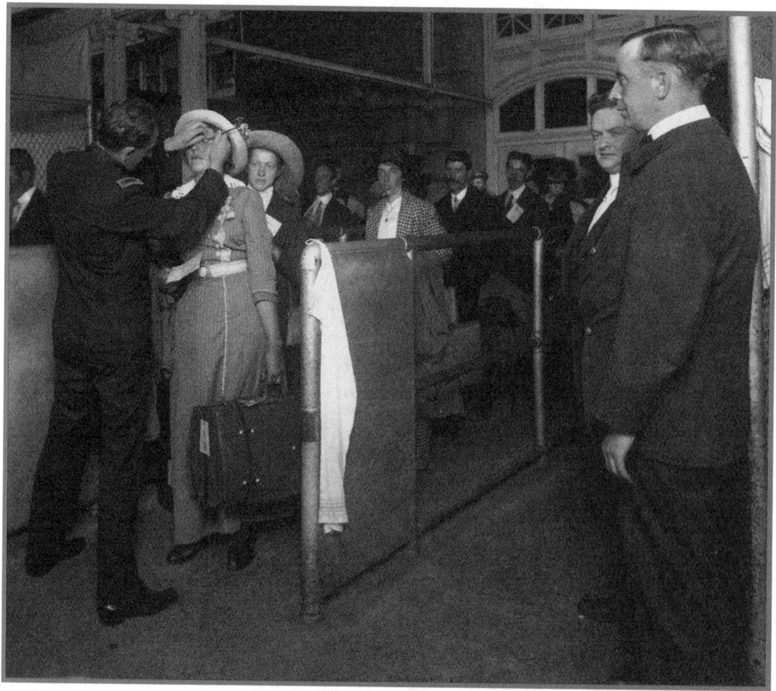

The Ellis Island Public Health Service doctors checked migrants for about 50 different health problems. For example, doctors examined immigrants for signs of trachoma, a highly contagious eye disease. Immigrants who had trachoma were usually deported.

understand that if her child had a few hours' rest and a little bite to eat she would be all right. In the end we did get through.

Mental Inspection

The most dreaded chalk mark of all was an "X." Immigrants marked with an "X" were thought to have mental problems.

Doctors used various kinds of tests to examine immigrants' intelligence. Sometimes the questions would make little sense to newcomers who didn't understand English very well. For example, doctors might ask questions such as, *Would you wash stairs from the top down or from the bottom up?*

About nine out of 100 immigrants were marked with an "X" during inspection. These people went to a special room for questioning. There, doctors asked a few personal questions, such as, "What is your name?" and "How old are you?" Then the doctors asked the person to count backwards, solve a math problem or puzzle, or copy a geometric shape. A Macedonian immigrant recalled,

> *The whole experience was very frightening. They brought me up to a room. They put a pegboard before me with little sticks of different shapes and little holes. I had to put them in place, the round ones and the square ones and I did it perfectly. They said "Oh, we must have made a mistake. This little girl . . . naturally she doesn't know English, but she's very bright, intelligent." They took the cross [chalk mark] off me so we were cleared.*

Legal Inspection

Immigrants who passed both the medical and mental exams moved on to wait for a legal inspection. An immigrant from Russia remembered:

> *Every so often somebody called out names of immigrants who were called in to be questioned. I was very nervous because it was so noisy. I couldn't hear the names and I was afraid that I would miss my name and remain there forever.*

Once their names were called, an inspector, with the help of an interpreter, asked many quick questions: *What is your name? What country are you from? Are you married or single? What is your occupation? Can you read or write? Have you ever been in prison? How much money do you have?*

These questions confirmed information recorded on steamship records. They were also supposed to determine whether immigrants were able to support themselves in the United States. The process took only a few minutes, after which an immigrant was either permitted to enter the United States or held for further questioning.

Most immigrants passed the tests. Then, they collected their baggage, exchanged their money for U.S. dollars, and waited outside for a ferry that would carry them to New York City—and a new life.

Heartbreak Island

As many as 20 percent of all immigrants coming through Ellis Island were **detained**, or held up, there for one reason or another. About two percent, or 250,000 of the 12 million who arrived over the years, were **deported**, or sent back, to Europe.

Sometimes families were held while waiting for money or tickets to arrive. Mothers and children waited for a husband or other relative to pick them up. When immigrants failed the medical exam, they and their families were detained until they grew healthy enough to leave. Ellis Island was a fearful place to be, especially for young children waiting for a sick parent to recover. Still, along with the fear, many remember acts of kindness. One immigrant, who arrived at age 12, has this fond memory,

> *There was a man that came around every morning and every afternoon, about ten o'clock in the morning and three o'clock in the afternoon, with a stainless-steel cart, sort of like a Good Humor cart, and he had warm milk for the kids. And they would blow a whistle or ring a bell and all the kids would line up. He had small little paper cups and he had a dipper and every kid got a little milk, warm milk. That was one thing that sticks in my mind.*

Immigrants with incurable diseases, or who failed the mental or legal exams, were usually deported as quickly as possible. Sometimes families were split apart. Mothers, fathers, grandparents, even children as young as ten years old, were sent back to Europe alone. For these people, Ellis Island became known as the "Isle of Tears" or "Heartbreak Island."

Thinking It Over

1. Why did immigrants dread the "X" chalk mark?
2. **Drawing Conclusions** Which immigrants were most likely to pass inspection without a problem?

Active Learning: Think about Ellis Island, the inspection process, and how it felt to wait to find out if you could enter the United States. Take additional notes for your letter, describing these experiences.

4 What Next?

After leaving New York, Renee Sidler settled in a small Connecticut town to begin work as a nanny. Her friend Marie traveled to the Midwest for her job as a maid. Of the 12 million people who came through Ellis Island, only one third remained in New York City. Eight million others traveled to areas across the country to places where industry was booming and jobs were easy to find.

The majority of immigrants traveled to their destinations by railway. They wore tags pinned to their clothing showing where they were traveling to and where they had to change trains. "Now that I think of it," recalls one woman, "we must have looked like marked-down merchandise in a department store."

Life in the City

Regardless of which part of the United States they chose, most immigrants settled in cities. By 1910, three out of four people in Boston, New York City, Chicago, Detroit, Cleveland, and other large cities were immigrants or children of immigrants.

Cities attracted immigrants for many reasons. Cities offered the most opportunities for work, because even unskilled laborers could find jobs in the factories. Cities also offered close ethnic neighborhoods, such as Little Italys, Chinatowns, and Germantowns. In these places, immigrants could speak their native languages, shop for ethnic foods, and keep traditional customs. Their neighborhoods bustled with energy, excitement, and feelings of familiarity.

However, this familiarity came at a price. Many immigrant neighborhoods were located in a city's poorer areas. Most families lived in **tenements**, crowded buildings with poor sanitation and safety, and little comfort. Before laws were passed calling for running water and a bathroom in each apartment, many families shared a hallway toilet and faucet with two or more other families.

Settling In

Immigrants faced other challenges as well. One was learning to speak English. Immigrants who spoke English had an easier time finding work, getting around town, and dealing with shopkeepers and landlords.

Often, parents relied on their children to do these things for them. Immigrant children learned English in school and quickly picked up American customs. They adjusted much more easily than their parents. A Lithuanian immigrant recalls,

> *It was kind of bad for awhile till we got to know people and speak the language. People say, you ought to preserve your own heritage or something, but all we could think of was, we didn't want to be different, we wanted to be like the rest of the Americans.*

Another challenge was that almost as soon as they entered the country, immigrants were encouraged to give up their old ways and speak,

Parents, children, and other relatives often lived together in tenement apartments. The front room served as the kitchen, washroom, and bedroom.

dress, and act American. While younger immigrants were often happy to oblige, older immigrants felt torn between their old customs and the new ones they were learning. Their feelings are best expressed by one Bulgarian immigrant. He says,

> *While I am not a whole American, neither am I what I was when I first landed here; that is, a Bulgarian. . . . In Bulgaria I am not wholly Bulgarian; in the United States, not wholly American.*

The End of an Era

Through the years, changes in immigration laws severely limited the number of immigrants who were allowed to enter the United States each year. There was another change—immigrants were now being checked at ports in the countries they were leaving. Immigration stations in the United States no longer examined newcomers, so there was not as much need for Ellis Island.

Ellis Island closed in 1954. In 1965, President Lyndon Johnson declared it a national monument. Today, Ellis Island is part of the Statue of Liberty/Ellis Island National Monument, which is run by the National Park Service. It stands as a museum of immigration history. About 40 percent of all Americans can trace their ancestry to immigrants arriving there.

Thinking It Over

1. Where did most immigrants settle?
2. **Making Inferences** Why do you think so many immigrants were drawn to ethnic neighborhoods?

Active Learning: Think about the thrills and challenges faced by newly arrived immigrants settling into the city. Take notes about what their homes and neighborhoods were like. Use this information to add a final paragraph to your letter.

GOING TO THE SOURCE

Passenger Lists

The United States government required steamship companies to keep lists of all their passengers. These lists provided a record of people arriving at U.S. immigration stations. These lists, called Manifests, contained each immigrant's name, age, birthplace, occupation, and other information. Upon arrival in New York, the steamship companies gave their Manifests to officials at Ellis Island. The officials used the names on the list to question immigrants during legal inspection. An example of a Manifest is shown below. Look at the Manifest, then answer the questions that follow.

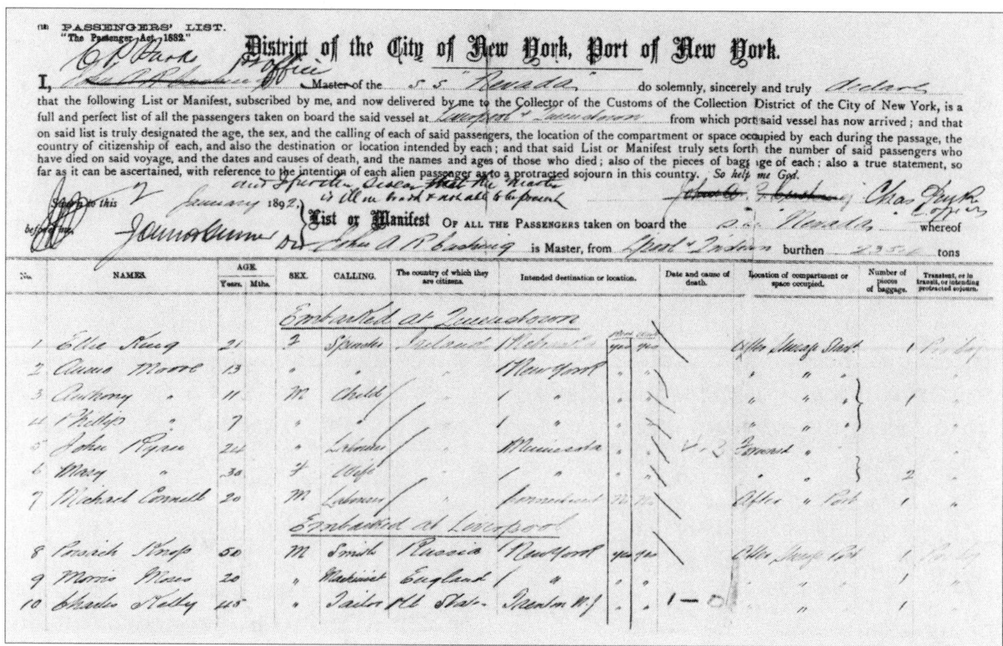

(18) PASSENGERS' LIST.
"The Passenger Act, 1882."

District of the City of New York, Port of New York.

I, [illegible], Master of the S. S. "Nevada" do solemnly, sincerely and truly declare that the following List or Manifest, subscribed by me, and now delivered by me to the Collector of the Customs of the Collection District of the City of New York, is a full and perfect list of all the passengers taken on board the said vessel at Liverpool & Queenstown from which port said vessel has now arrived; and that on said list is truly designated the age, the sex, and the calling of each of said passengers, the location of the compartment or space occupied by each during the passage, the country of citizenship of each, and also the destination or location intended by each; and that said List or Manifest truly sets forth the number of said passengers who have died on said voyage, and the dates and causes of death, and the names and ages of those who died; also of the pieces of baggage of each; also a true statement, so far as it can be ascertained, with reference to the intention of each alien passenger as to a protracted sojourn in this country. *So help me God.*

Sworn to this 2 January 1892, before me. [illegible]

List or Manifest OF ALL THE PASSENGERS taken on board the S. S. Nevada whereof John A. P. [illegible] is Master, from Liverpool & Queenstown burthen [illegible] tons

No.	NAMES.	AGE. Years.	AGE. Mths.	SEX.	CALLING.	The country of which they are citizens.	Intended destination or location.	Date and cause of death.	Location of compartment or space occupied.	Number of pieces of baggage.	Transient, or in transit, or intending protracted sojourn.
	Embarked at Queenstown										
1	Ellie King	21		F	Spinster	Ireland	Nebraska		After Steerage Std.	1	[illegible]
2	Annie Moore	13		"	"	"	New York		" "		"
3	Anthony "	11		M	Child	"	" "		" "	1	"
4	Phillip "	7		"	"	"	" "		" "		"
5	John Ryan	24		"	Laborer	"	Minnesota		Forward "		"
6	Mary "	30		F	Wife	"	" "		" "	2	"
7	Michael Connell	20		M	Laborer	"	Connecticut		After " Port	1	"
	Embarked at Liverpool										
8	[illegible]	50		M	Smith	Russia	New York		After Steerage Port	1	[illegible]
9	Morris Moses	20		"	Machinist	England	" "		" "	1	"
10	Charles Kelly	45		"	Tailor	[illegible]	Trenton N.J.		"	1	"

1. What was the purpose of the Manifest?
2. **Analyzing** What are some questions that inspectors might have asked based on the information provided in the Manifest?

Case Study Review

Identifying Main Ideas

1. What conditions did most immigrants encounter on their voyages to the United States?
2. What kinds of inspections did immigrants undergo at Ellis Island?
3. What advantages and disadvantages did cities offer to immigrants?

Working Together

Form a small group with three or four students. Use the information in this case study and other resources from your school or local library to create a bulletin board display about the immigrant experience. Include quotes from people who experienced related events; this case study contains a number of these quotes. Once you decide which quotes you would like to use, find pictures or create drawings to portray those experiences.

Active Learning

Writing a Letter Review the notes you wrote as you read this case study. Organize them so that they create a clear picture of your experiences as a newly arrived immigrant in America. Add information if you need more details. You should include a description of what life was like in steerage, what you went through at Ellis Island, and what it is like to live in a large city. After you organize your letter, read it. It should read as if you are writing to family members "back home" in Europe.

Lessons for Today

For many years, immigrants were encouraged to give up their ethnic customs and to adopt American ones. Many people believed Americans should all be the same. Today more and more people are rejecting that idea. They want to focus on what makes them unique. Do you think it is difficult for people to hold on to different cultural traditions once they become Americans? Write a brief essay explaining your point of view.

What Might You Have Done?

Service organizations and volunteers offered classes and activities to help immigrants adjust to life in America and to provide relief from their harsh living conditions. What might you have done to help immigrants face challenges in the United States?

CRITICAL THINKING

Analyzing a Poem

The Language of Thinking

Analyzing is part of the learning process. When you analyze something, you break it into its parts in order to examine it more closely. Analyzing information allows you to understand events or issues better.

Poets pack a lot of meaning into a small amount of space. They choose each word of a poem carefully so that, when put together, the words create strong images or evoke strong emotions. The following poem, "The New Colossus" by Emma Lazarus, appears on the base of The Statue of Liberty. Read it and then answer the questions below.

Not like the brazen giant of Greek fame,
With conquering limbs astride from land to land,
Here at our sea-washed, sunset gates shall stand
A mighty woman with a torch, whose flame
Is the imprisoned lightning, and her name
Mother of Exiles. From her beacon-hand
Glows world-wide welcome; her mild eyes command
The air-bridged harbor that twin cities frame.
"Keep ancient lands, your storied pomp!" cries she
With silent lips. "Give me your tired, your poor,
Your huddled masses yearning to breathe free,
The wretched refuse of your teeming shore.
Send these, the homeless, tempest-tost to me,
I lift my lamp beside the golden door!"

1. **Interpreting Details** What words does the author use to portray those seeking a new life in America? Do you think those words apply to immigrants in the early 1900s? Do they apply today?
2. **Analyzing** What might be some meanings for the words "golden door"?

Their traditional clothing set the Chinese apart and added to the prejudice many native-born Americans felt toward them.

CASE STUDY 2

CONNECTING THE COASTS

CRITICAL QUESTIONS

- What part did Chinese immigrants play in the building of the first transcontinental railroad?
- What restrictions did the United States place on Chinese immigrants during the late 1800s?

TERMS TO KNOW

- avalanches
- transcontinental
- Homestead Act
- Pacific Railway Act
- provinces
- trestles
- nitroglycerin
- Chinese Exclusion Act
- certificate of residence
- Chinatowns
- fongs

ACTIVE LEARNING

In this case study, you will learn about the contributions and sacrifices Chinese immigrants made in building the transcontinental railroad. At the end of the case study, you will prepare a speech honoring their hard work and dedication. Use the suggestions in the Active Learning boxes to help you prepare your assignment.

The winter of 1866–67 was brutally cold, especially high up in the Sierra Nevada mountains of eastern California. There, more than 6,000 Chinese laborers, using only pickaxes and shovels, chipped away at great walls of solid rock. Throughout the winter, they used dynamite to blast tunnels through which great steam trains would one day travel.

Snow fell constantly, covering the workers' camps and building sites. At times, explosions of dynamite caused **avalanches**, blankets of snow that slid through the camps, sweeping workers to an icy death in the canyon below.

Still, the construction bosses insisted that the Chinese continue. At first, the men dug paths in the snow from their camps to the tunnels. When that became impossible, they lived and worked in the cold tunnels, beneath snowdrifts up to 60 feet tall. They used lanterns for light and dug shafts to let in fresh air.

When spring finally brought relief from the harsh winter weather, railroad bosses gave workers a surprise. They increased the workday from eight hours to twelve and the workweek from six days to seven. They felt that the job was taking too long and urged the men to work longer and faster.

For their grueling work, the Chinese were paid $31 per month. White workers were paid that amount plus board and lodging, which added an additional $10 to their wages. Although construction bosses offered the Chinese a small increase in wages, the workers were not satisfied. They demanded to be paid the same amount and wanted to work the same number of hours as white workers. When the bosses refused, the Chinese went on strike—almost all stayed in their camps and refused to work.

However, the Chinese depended on the railroad company for food and other supplies. They were working far from towns and cities and had no place to go. The railroad bosses knew this and immediately cut off the workers' food supply. Within a week, the isolated and starving strikers gave up and went back to work.

A Good Book to Read

Dragon's Gate, by Laurence Yep. New York: HarperTrophy, 1995.

From rural China in 1865, Otter, a teenage boy, eagerly sails to California to join his father who is working on the transcontinental railroad. Otter's dreams are shattered when he joins the crew and experiences brutal cold, dangerous work, and other hardships.

1 A Growing Country

In the mid 1800s, the United States was rapidly expanding. At the start of the Civil War, there were 35,000 miles of railroad track in the United States, most of them in the Northeast. Railroads made travel and trade both easier and faster, and they enabled communities to develop in previously remote areas. However, the vast stretch of land between Nebraska and California had not yet been developed. Travel and trade between communities in the far West and communities in the East remained slow. People and goods usually traveled on wagon trains to cities and towns in the West.

Community leaders throughout the United States began pushing for a **transcontinental** railroad, a railroad that would extend across the continent, connecting the country's east and west coasts. Such a railroad, they felt, was a matter of national importance. It would open up western lands to farmers, allow miners to transport gold and other resources east, and expand opportunities for communication, travel, and trade within the entire country.

The Pacific Railway Act

In 1862, the same year that Congress passed the **Homestead Act**, a law that allowed citizens and permanent immigrants to claim 160 acres of public land for a $10 fee, President Abraham Lincoln signed into law the **Pacific Railway Act**. The Pacific Railway Act provided for the building of the transcontinental railroad. The two laws were connected, because the building of the railroad would allow people to claim land more easily and thus develop communities in the West.

Building the transcontinental railroad would be the greatest engineering feat the nation had ever attempted, and two major railroad companies would share the responsibility. The Union Pacific Railroad, based in the east, would build toward the west from Omaha, Nebraska. The Central Pacific Railroad, based in California, would build toward the east from Sacramento, California. When the two railroad companies met, the transcontinental railroad would be complete.

After the passage of the law, the U.S. government encouraged railroad construction and competition in several ways. The government provided loans of about $65 million to the companies. In order to increase competition, the government agreed to pay each company based on the number of miles of track that was laid. Each mile of track would be worth payments of hundreds of thousands of dollars. The U.S. government also promised to give away public land. For each mile of track laid, a railroad company received 10 square miles of land; this total was later increased to 20 square miles.

Besides having to do backbreaking physical labor, railroad workers struggled against heat, dust, blizzards, and floods.

The Search for Workers

Five partners owned the Central Pacific Railroad. Together they raised the money and bought the equipment that was needed to begin work. By the end of 1862, they were ready to start.

Charles Crocker was the owner in charge of construction. He hired laborers to lay the tracks and build the bridges. At first, hiring proved difficult, because most of the men in California were busy mining for gold, which had been discovered in the area in 1848. Railroad work was hard and lonely; men had to live in camps, separated from families and friends for months or years at a time. Those who signed on with the Central Pacific often quit after a few weeks.

Crocker grew desperate. The Union Pacific Railroad had plenty of workers, mostly ex-Civil War soldiers and recently arrived immigrants from Ireland. They were already laying track well into the state of Nebraska.

For a long time, Crocker refused to consider one source of available labor—the Chinese. He felt that Chinese workers were too small and too weak to do the hard work of blasting through the solid granite of the Sierras, laying track, and building bridges. Finally, Crocker decided to give the Chinese a try.

Thinking It Over

1. What was the Pacific Railway Act?
2. **Drawing Conclusions** Why do you think the federal government encouraged competition in building the transcontinental railroad?

2 An Army of Immigrants

By the time the Pacific Railway Act went into effect, thousands of Chinese were already living in California. Many had left China during the 1850s to escape wars and internal rebellions against the Chinese government. One such uprising, the Taiping Rebellion, started in 1850 and lasted 14 years, killing millions of people and creating areas of severe poverty. Even though emigration was a crime punishable by death, many Chinese fled to other countries. When they heard that gold had been discovered in California, many were eager to come to the United States.

Some Chinese who came were skilled workers, such as doctors, engineers, iron smiths, and carpenters. They came not to mine but to provide services to the miners. Most, however, were young, poorly educated farmers and fishermen hoping to strike it rich. They came from the **provinces**, or territories, of Kwangtung and Fujian, areas that had more people than could be fed as well as frequent, crop-ruining floods. The men planned to stay in the United States just long enough to make enough money to support their families; then they would return to China and buy land there.

Chinese who had come to the United States and then returned to their villages in China inspired others to come. They called the United States *Gum Shan*—"the mountain of gold."

In Search of Gold Mountain

Before 1848, fewer than 1,000 Chinese lived in the United States; only 54 were in California. Once the gold rush started, the numbers increased rapidly. Between 1850 and 1860, more than 60,000 Chinese made their way across the Pacific Ocean to the United States. Most of them settled in California. This steady immigration continued until 1876. By that time there were about 150,000 Chinese in the United States—116,000 in California alone.

In the 1850s and 1860s, there were no immigration laws, so people could enter and leave the United States without restriction. At the height of the gold rush, foreign shipping companies, hoping to profit by carrying Chinese immigrants to the gold mines, raised the cost of passage from China to the United States from $40 to as high as $200. They distributed advertisements in China's port cities, promising opportunities to strike it rich in California. One such flyer stated,

> *Americans are very rich people. They want the Chinamen to come and make him very welcome. There you will have great pay, large houses, and food and clothing of the finest description. . . . It is a nice country. . . . Money is in great plenty and to spare in America.*

At first, the Chinese seemed welcome in the United States. The Chinese worked for low wages, while whites worked at getting rich in the gold fields. The Chinese quickly became carpenters, cooks, and farmers. Newspapers and politicians spoke kindly of them. A reporter in one newspaper, the *Alta California*, wrote,

> *These [Chinese] make excellent citizens and we are pleased to notice their daily arrival in large numbers.*

Competition for Gold

However, their welcome did not last long. The Chinese soon experienced hostility from white Americans, who resented their presence in the mines and in other industries. In reality, the Chinese did not compete with white miners. Most Chinese did not pan for gold in the streams the way white miners did. They usually dug the remaining gold dust from an old mine, finding gold where other miners had given up. They also used a special device called a Chinese waterwheel to dredge gold out of streams that other miners had abandoned.

White and Chinese miners were friendly as long as there was plenty of undiscovered gold. When finding new sources of gold started to become rare, bitter white miners blamed the Chinese for taking all the gold. Their slogan became "California for the Americans."

Attacks Against the Chinese

In 1850, California passed the Foreign Miners' License law—a tax of $20 a month on foreign miners. The result was that many Chinese left the mining camps and went to the cities to find work. San Francisco filled up with very poor immigrants. The law was removed in 1851.

One of the earliest to attack the Chinese in California was John Bigler, the state's first governor. During his campaign for office, Bigler had supported Chinese immigration. Then, in running for reelection, he realized that many white people resented how successful the Chinese had become. He also realized that the Chinese could not vote. In 1852, he spoke out against the Chinese in a speech to the state legislature. He said that European immigration was beneficial to the state but that Chinese immigration was not. He argued that the Chinese did not fit in with Americans and that they were immoral, greedy, and dangerous. He concluded that Chinese immigration should be stopped.

Many Chinese answered the governor's criticism through letters to newspapers. The Chinese also published their own newspaper, *The Orient,* in both English and Chinese.

When Governor Bigler continued his anti-Chinese attack, a group of Chinese merchants that called itself the Committee of Chinese wrote an answer to him in *The Orient*. It pointed out that if Americans went to China, they would not be able to speak the language immediately or adjust quickly to the local customs, yet it would be unfair for the Chinese not to accept these Americans. The letter showed that Bigler's complaints were completely false. The letter also stated that if white Americans continued to treat the Chinese in such a racist way, these immigrants should pack up and return to China.

California's Anti-Chinese Laws

In spite of protests from the Chinese, the California legislature passed several anti-Chinese laws. For example, the Foreign Miners' Tax in 1852 forced all miners who were not citizens to pay a tax of $3 a month. A year later the tax was increased to $4 a month. The tax was aimed specifically at the Chinese, who couldn't become citizens even if they had wanted to. A 1790 law allowed only white immigrants to apply for citizenship.

According to the law, tax collectors could take the property of anyone who did not pay the tax and sell it as payment for the tax. These tax collectors were also paid according to how much tax money they could collect, so they would often force the same miners to pay the tax several times each month.

By 1870, more than 100,000 Chinese had come to the United States. Most were men who hoped to earn money in the United States and then return to their families in China.

In 1855, California added another tax, called the Immigrant Tax. Its goal was to "discourage the immigration to this state of persons who cannot become citizens thereof"—the Chinese.

The Chinese could not even fight back against discrimination or unfair taxes in court because they weren't allowed to testify in court. In 1854, in the case of *People v. Hall*, the California Supreme Court ruled that only white people could testify against white defendants in a criminal case. In 1863, a California state law extended the court ruling to cover all kinds of court cases.

As less and less gold was discovered, many white miners left the gold fields and went to the cities to find work. The booming California economy, which had been based on gold discoveries, now went sour. Businesses failed and unemployment soared. Suddenly there were many more workers than there were jobs. These unemployed whites looked at the Chinese as the source of their troubles. They claimed that the Chinese had taken jobs away from white workers because they would work for low wages and that the Chinese took money away from the community by sending their savings back to their families in China.

Thinking It Over

1. What were some of the anti-Chinese laws passed by the California legislature?
2. **Analyzing** Why do you think white miners blamed the Chinese, and not other immigrant groups, for their troubles?

Active Learning: As you read, take notes on how the Chinese were treated in California. You can use some of this information in your speech.

3 From Gold Mines to Railroads

Year by year, the Chinese were forced out of mining and had to seek other types of labor. Some returned to China, but many could not afford the cost of passage. Those who stayed needed money to send back to their families, so they found jobs as house servants, in restaurants, or as general laborers.

In February 1865, the Central Pacific Railroad hired 50 Chinese workers on a trial basis. The other workers were outraged. They ranted and jeered as the Chinese quietly set up camp in the mountains, boiled rice for supper, and went to sleep.

At dawn, the Chinese were up and ready to work. With picks and shovels in hand, they worked straight through the day, moving in teams to complete each task. Every few hours they took a break to drink hot tea, then they went right back to work. At the end of the day, Crocker could see that the Chinese had worked harder and gotten more done than the white laborers.

Even Central Pacific president Leland Stanford, who had been elected governor of California on a promise to stop Chinese immigration, now described the Chinese workers as "quiet, peaceable, industrious, economical." Within two months, his company hired more than 2,000 Chinese workers. When the other workers threatened to quit and demanded that Central Pacific hire only white men, Crocker replied,

> *We can't get enough white labor to build this railroad, and build it we must, so we're forced to hire them. If you can't get along with them, we have only one alternative. We'll let you go and hire nobody but them.*

The Chinese proved that they could meet the superhuman task of building the transcontinental railroad. For example, on April 28, 1869, the Chinese set a new record for laying track. They were determined to beat the record of eight miles of track in one day that had been set by Irish workers on the competing Union Pacific Railroad. At the end of that workday, the Chinese had lifted 1,000 tons of steel and laid 10 miles of track in 12 hours.

Once the owners of the Central Pacific Railroad discovered how valuable Chinese workers were, they signed up as many as they could find. Before long, labor agents went directly to China to bring back more, paying their fares and then deducting the cost from their wages once they were in the United States.

Many Chinese eagerly took jobs building the railroad. In California, a Chinese railroad worker could earn $30 per month. In China, a worker could make about $3 to $5 dollars per month.

Dangerous Work

By mid-1866, more than 6,000 Chinese were working on the Central Pacific. Within two years, that number climbed to 12,000, accounting for 90 percent of Central Pacific's entire work force.

But working on the railroad was not easy. Most days were spent toiling in either blazing heat or brutal cold. Workers laid track through rugged mountains and over miles of desert. They leveled hills, cleared trees, and filled gorges with dirt so that ties could be laid evenly along the trail. They shoveled, drilled, and carted rocks and earth. They built countless **trestles**, or bridges, for trains to travel across.

The Chinese also did jobs that no one else would do. They dangled over the edges of snow-covered cliffs to insert sticks of dynamite into holes in the mountainside. After lighting the dynamite, other workers would yank them up and away from the blast—though they didn't always make it.

Chinese workers also handled **nitroglycerin**, an explosive liquid that other workers would not touch. They used the liquid to blast tunnels through solid rock. On one 42-mile path through the highest peaks of the Sierra Nevada mountains, they built 18 tunnels. Even the white co-workers who had originally harassed the Chinese came to admire their hard work.

Although the Chinese railroad workers took many risks in their work, they were very careful in their camp routines. They washed daily and, unlike other workers who lived on a diet of company-supplied beef, beans, potatoes, and coffee, they set up their own kitchens. They demanded that their own food be transported by wagon train from San Francisco. They ate a healthy diet of dried fish, noodles, dried bamboo shoots, dried fruit, vegetables, rice, and tea. The tea was always made with boiled water, while white workers drank unboiled water.

These habits protected them from sicknesses such as dysentery and scurvy that often affected white workers. At one point, working at a height of 7,000 feet, many white workers became sick or quit, but the Chinese kept going.

Chinese laborers conquered California's Sierra Nevada Mountains. The tracks they laid on trestles such as this one extended over gorges and across rivers.

The Final Spikes Are Driven

By the spring of 1868, the Central Pacific workers had made it through the Sierra Nevada mountains. Now working on smoother landscape, they moved with greater speed. Mile by mile, across Nevada and into Utah, they rapidly approached the competing Union Pacific Railroad.

As the two companies drew closer, they worked faster and faster, completing two and three miles of track per day. Finally, in the spring of 1869, the Central Pacific met the Union Pacific at Promontory Point, Utah. On May 10, 1869, the railroad owners drove the final gold and silver spikes into the rail. A telegraph operator beside the tracks sent the message: "Dot . . . Dot . . . Done."

Thinking It Over

1. What opportunities brought Chinese immigrants to California?
2. **Making Inferences** How do you think the daily camp routines of Chinese workers influenced their ability to get the job done?

An Act of Betrayal

With the completion of the transcontinental railroad, thousands of Chinese laborers were suddenly out of work. Some returned home to China, some went to Canada to help build the Canadian Pacific Railroad, and some worked on smaller railroads in California and other western states. Most headed toward San Francisco in search of other jobs. Between 1860 and 1870, San Francisco's Chinese population swelled from 2,700 to more than 12,000—out of a total of 63,000 Chinese immigrants in the United States. San Francisco was the largest center of Chinese people in the United States.

Many Chinese found work in factories, making boots, shoes, clothing, and cigars. By 1870, Chinese made up about 75 percent of San Francisco's woolen-mill workers and 90 percent of the city's cigar makers. Some found work in fishing and canning industries along the Pacific coast from California to Alaska. Others worked in the agricultural industry, where they used their past experiences of farming in China to turn the swamps of California's San Joaquin and Sacramento River deltas into rich, productive farmland.

When the Central Pacific Railroad and the Union Pacific Railroad linked in Utah, no Chinese were shown in the photo taken of the event.

The Chinese built levees and dikes in California's Sacramento and San Joaquin river valleys to turn swampland into fertile soil. In the 1880s, three out of four farm workers in California were Chinese.

Before long, more white laborers—both native born and immigrant—found themselves in competition with Chinese workers, and they didn't like it. Their frustration grew as jobs became harder to find.

Growing Resentment Against the Chinese

During the 1870s, many western states were in an economic depression that was caused by a severe drought, crop failures, and less and less gold produced from mines. Many businesses failed, putting thousands of men and women out of work. White workers felt that the Chinese were taking the few jobs that were available. They also felt that because Chinese workers earned less than whites, they were holding down wages.

White workers in San Francisco and other California towns protested against the Chinese. At this time, a major leader in the anti-Chinese movement was Denis Kearney, an Irish immigrant. He was the leader of the Workingmen's Party, a political party that controlled the California legislature. He often supported violence against the Chinese and ended his speeches with "The Chinese must go!" As Kearney said,

> *There is no means left to clear the Chinamen but to swing them into eternity by their own queues [pigtails], for there is no rope long enough in all America wherewith to strangle four hundred millions of Chinamen.*

Throughout the country, whites threatened Chinese workers. Resentment that had been simmering since the Chinese first started arriving in the United States 20 years earlier erupted in anti-Chinese riots and violence. Recalls Chinese immigrant Andrew Kan,

> *We were simply terrified; we kept indoors after dark for fear of being shot in the back. Children spit upon us as we passed by and called us rats.*

At times, Chinese workers were dragged to trains and forced out of town. Anti-Chinese riots spread from California to Colorado, Montana, and Nevada. In October 1871, a mob in Los Angeles shot, hanged, and stabbed 19 Chinese to death. Members of the mob also destroyed Chinese stores and homes. In July 1877, a riot in San Francisco lasted 3 days and resulted in the burning of dozens of Chinese businesses and homes. In September 1885, white coal miners attacked 500 Chinese miners in Rock Springs, Wyoming. They killed 28 Chinese and wounded 15 others, searching and robbing valuables from those who were shot. All the Chinese houses were burned, causing more than $140,000 in damages.

Of course, anti-Chinese feelings weren't always job related. The Chinese were different in appearance, culture, and religion. The Chinese usually wore blue cotton shirts, baggy pants, quilted jackets, and basket-like hats. They shaved the front of their heads and wore their hair in long queues that hung down the backs of their necks.

White workers could not understand or accept these differences. Even other immigrants considered the Chinese as "outsiders."

Legalized Discrimination

Whatever the reasons, the anti-Chinese movement grew more and more powerful. Workers formed organizations that pressured lawmakers into restricting Chinese immigration. Politicians, eager to gain votes, made anti-Chinese speeches.

In 1879, the new California constitution banned anyone except native-born whites, white immigrants, and African Americans from owning or inheriting land. The next year, the legislature passed a law that stopped immigrants from fishing or selling fish taken from California waters.

In addition, the Board of Supervisors in San Francisco passed several city laws against the Chinese. In 1870, the Cubic Air Law required every house to have at least 500 cubic feet of air per person living there. The fine for breaking the law was $10 to $50 plus 5 days to 3 months in jail. Because many Chinese lived in cramped housing, they were arrested and jailed.

In 1876, the Queue Ordinance allowed the sheriff to cut the hair of all male prisoners to within one inch of the scalp. The Qing Dynasty, the rulers in China, required all Chinese men to wear their hair in queues to show respect for the emperor. It was considered a disgrace to lose one's queue. Three years later, the U.S. Circuit Court ruled that the ordinance was unconstitutional.

In 1879, the Laundry Ordinance made laundry owners pay special fees. Any laundry using a horse-drawn wagon was charged $2 every 3 months; the owner of two wagons had to pay $4. However, a laundry owner who owned no wagons was forced to pay $15. Chinese laundry owners never used wagons.

On a national level, both Republican and Democratic politicians took stands against the Chinese. In 1882, Congress passed the **Chinese Exclusion Act**, which banned immigration of Chinese laborers for the next 10 years and denied citizenship to Chinese already living here. As the first national law that specifically discriminated against a particular immigrant group, it marked a turning point in U.S. immigration policy. Another national law declared that if a white female American citizen married a Chinese living in the United States, she would lose her U.S. citizenship.

Many states used the intent of the Chinese Exclusion Act to pass their own discrimination laws against the Chinese. In Montana, for example, lawmakers declared that anyone who could not become a U.S. citizen could not own a mine. Some states banned marriage between Chinese and whites. Similar laws that discriminated against the Chinese were passed in other areas of the United States. As a result, many Chinese lost their businesses, their jobs, and their land.

In 1910, as part of this restrictive immigration policy, the U.S. government built a detention center on Angel Island in San Francisco Bay. There, immigrants were held temporarily while officials examined their claims to prior residence or of a relationship with U.S. citizens. Angel Island became a prison for hundreds of Chinese, where immigrants, separated from their families, were detained from 2 weeks to as long as 22 months. This detention center was not closed until 1940.

Active Learning: You have just read about threats, violence, and laws against the Chinese. Take notes on this history of undeserved treatment and add them to your speech.

Tighter Laws

Threats and violence against the Chinese increased greatly after the Chinese Exclusion Act. Books, magazines, and newspapers described the Chinese as evil and claimed that they threatened American life. Growing fears and prejudices among citizens led to even greater restrictions against the Chinese.

Although the Chinese Exclusion Act of 1882 had protected the right of Chinese immigrants already living in the United States to travel freely to and from the country, the Scott Act of 1888 took that right away. When the law passed, more than 20,000 Chinese laborers were temporarily out of the country. They could not return—even if they had certificates guaranteeing that they could. That year, only 26 Chinese immigrants entered the United States. The new law separated many families.

In 1892, laws became even tighter. Every Chinese person living in the United States had to carry a **certificate of residence**, a special document proving that he or she was in the country legally. Also in 1892, the Geary Act renewed the Chinese Exclusion Act for another 10 years. In 1902, Congress extended it indefinitely.

Finally, in 1924, the National Origins Act drastically restricted immigration to the United States from every country in Asia. Even the wives and children of Chinese merchants and American-born Chinese could no longer come to the United States. With a quota of about 100 people per year, this law cut off Chinese immigration almost completely. From that point on, the number of Chinese in the United States gradually decreased, as many immigrants returned home or moved to friendlier nations.

Thinking It Over

1. What effects did the anti-Chinese laws have on Chinese life in this country?
2. **Drawing Conclusions** Why do you think the Exclusion Act led to increased violence against Chinese immigrants already living in the United States?

5 A Changing Community

Long before prejudice against the Chinese became widespread, they had formed their own communities. Most moved from rural areas to cities, where they lived and worked in ethnic neighborhoods, called **Chinatowns**. These communities developed in cities both large and small throughout the United States.

In Chinatowns, the Chinese could exist without fear. They could speak their own language,

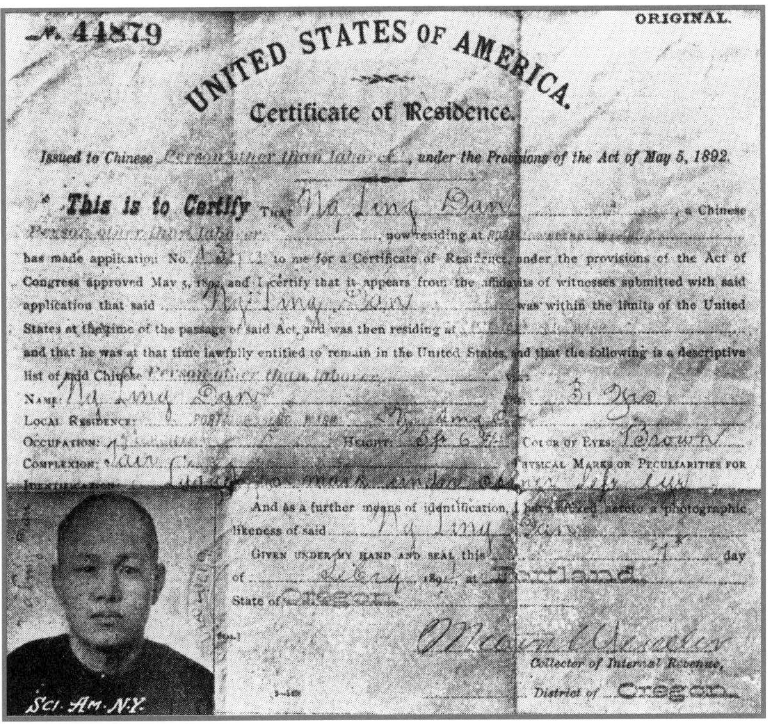

No. 44879 ORIGINAL.

UNITED STATES OF AMERICA.

Certificate of Residence.

Issued to Chinese Person other than laborer, *under the Provisions of the Act of May 5, 1892.*

This is to Certify THAT Ng Ling Dan, a Chinese Person other than laborer, now residing at [illegible] has made application No. [illegible] to me for a Certificate of Residence under the provisions of the Act of Congress approved May 5, 1892, and I certify that it appears from the affidavits of witnesses submitted with said application that said Ng Ling Dan was within the limits of the United States at the time of the passage of said Act, and was then residing at [illegible] and that he was at that time lawfully entitled to remain in the United States, and that the following is a descriptive list of said Chinese Person other than laborer viz:

NAME: Ng Ling Dan AGE: 51 yrs

LOCAL RESIDENCE: [illegible]

OCCUPATION: [illegible] HEIGHT: 5 ft 6 ¾ COLOR OF EYES: Brown

COMPLEXION: [illegible] PHYSICAL MARKS OR PECULIARITIES FOR IDENTIFICATION: [illegible]

And as a further means of identification, I have affixed hereto a photographic likeness of said Ng Ling Dan.

GIVEN UNDER MY HAND AND SEAL this [illegible] day of [illegible] 189[illegible], at Portland State of Oregon.

[signature]

Collector of Internal Revenue,

District of Oregon.

Anti-Chinese feeling in the United States led to the passage of the Chinese Exclusion Act, which required Chinese living in this country to carry certificates of residence.

eat traditional foods, buy traditional clothing, and carry on the customs they had brought from China. By 1900, Chinatowns had developed in many U.S. cities. One Chinatown resident recalled,

> *Most of us can live a warmer, freer, and more humane life among our relatives and friends than among strangers.*

For the most part, Chinatowns were bachelor societies. When Chinese men had first come to the United States, most were married, but according to Chinese custom, their wives and children had stayed behind in China. Of the 11,794 Chinese that came to California in 1852, only seven were women. Later immigration laws made it almost impossible for men to bring their families to the United States. By 1870, the ratio of Chinese men to Chinese women was 14 to 1. In 1900, about 95 percent of Chinese Americans were male. Some merchants brought their wives, but the women lived secluded lives, according to Chinese tradition.

Separated from their wives and unable to return to China, many men were forced to remain single, supporting their families from afar. One Chinese American writer remarked,

> *In every Chinese American family history there are stories of lives made miserable by the immigration laws, harassment, and fear: the lonely old single men in condemned hotel rooms, the suicides of deportees, the fragmented families.*

As violence against the Chinese increased, Chinatowns became the only safe havens. Within the confines of their neighborhoods, Chinese took refuge and continued their separate culture.

Fighting Back

Although the Chinese sought safety in Chinatowns, they did not quietly accept discrimination. In San Francisco's Chinatown, an organization called Chung Wah Kung Saw, or the Chinese Consolidated Benevolent Association (CCBA), became the major voice for the Chinese people. This organization was also called the Six Companies, because it represented six geographical areas of China where immigrants had once lived.

Originally formed in the 1850s, the CCBA was the informal government for San Francisco's Chinatown. It served the community by opening a school for Chinese children, arranging return passages to China, and fighting against prejudice and discrimination by bringing cases to court. The CCBA had branches in many cities.

Another organization in Chinatown was known as the tongs. These were secret societies whose members were engaged in illegal activities, such as gambling and drug dealing. Using hatchets and knives, groups of tongs would sometimes battle one another on the streets of Chinatown.

In 1924, some Chinese, who were not satisfied with the work of the CCBA, formed the Native Sons of the Golden State. This organization, which became the Chinese American Citizens Alliance, still continues to fight against prejudice.

New Opportunities

The Chinese also fought back by helping one another. They employed each other in their stores and restaurants. In addition, they developed social centers, called **fongs**, that ran clubs and provided jobs, housing, and other opportunities.

When growing resentment forced the Chinese from factory and other jobs, they established their own businesses—such as laundries, stores, and restaurants—that did not compete with American businesses. More and more Chinese worked in these types of jobs. For example, the first Chinese American laundry was opened in 1851 by Wah Lee in San Francisco. He charged $5 to wash and iron a dozen shirts. Twenty years later, there were 2,000 laundries in San Francisco. By 1890, there were 6,400 Chinese laundry workers in California; this total represented almost 70 percent of all laundry workers in the United States.

A Long Road

Laws against Chinese immigrants lasted until World War II. During the war, China and the United States fought as allies. President Franklin Roosevelt asked Congress to repeal the Chinese Exclusion Act, and in 1943, Congress complied, granting naturalization rights to all foreign-born Chinese.

After World War II, the nature of Chinese immigration changed. By then, about 90 percent of new Chinese immigrants were women—the wives of American servicemen and wives joining their husbands in the United States. For the first time, families developed in Chinatown.

In the 1950s and 1960s, the United States welcomed refugees from the communist regime in China and provided scholarships for Chinese students to enable them to study at American colleges. Since the 1960s, new laws have allowed about 20,000 Chinese to emigrate each year.

Throughout the 1970s, the Chinese began to leave Chinatowns and move into the middle-class suburbs of some cities. They also exercised their voting power to elect Chinese American politicians to local governments, such as Lily Chen, who was elected as the first Chinese mayor of Monterey Park, California, in the 1980s. Chinese Americans have also formed feminist and antiwar groups that have taken part in demonstrations.

In addition, Chinese Americans have been recognized for their creative ability. For example, Arabella Hong was the first Chinese American to play a leading role in a Broadway show when she performed in *Flower Drum Song*. Maxine Hong Kingston and Amy Tan are two well-known Chinese American authors, whose best-selling books concern the struggles of Chinese American families. Wayne Wang, a Chinese American moviemaker, turned Amy Tan's *The Joy Luck Club* into a popular film. Connie Chung, a Chinese American TV journalist, has been the cohost of several national news programs. I.M. Pei, a Chinese American architect, designed the John F. Kennedy library in Boston and the Rock and Roll Hall of Fame in Cleveland. Yo-Yo Ma, a Chinese American musician, is recognized as one of the greatest living cellists.

Today, Chinese Americans number over one million. Each year thousands more take the oath of naturalization. Even though their roots stretch back to the ancient traditions of China, they have contributed their talents to enrich American society.

Thinking It Over

1. How did anti-Chinese sentiment affect where Chinese immigrants lived and worked in the United States?
2. **Analyzing** Why do you think Chinese immigrants felt safer in Chinatowns?

The population of many Western towns was mainly male. The Chinese who set up laundries in these towns became successful businessowners. By 1920, the majority of Chinese in the United States worked in laundries or restaurants.

GOING TO THE SOURCE

Come to California

In the late 1800s, laborers, unions, and politicians—especially those based in California—were calling for tighter controls on Chinese immigration. They claimed there were not enough jobs to go around. Yet, only three years after Congress passed the Chinese Exclusion Act, the California Immigration Commission of the Central Pacific Railroad passed out this booklet to attract immigrants to California. Look at the booklet, and then answer the questions that follow.

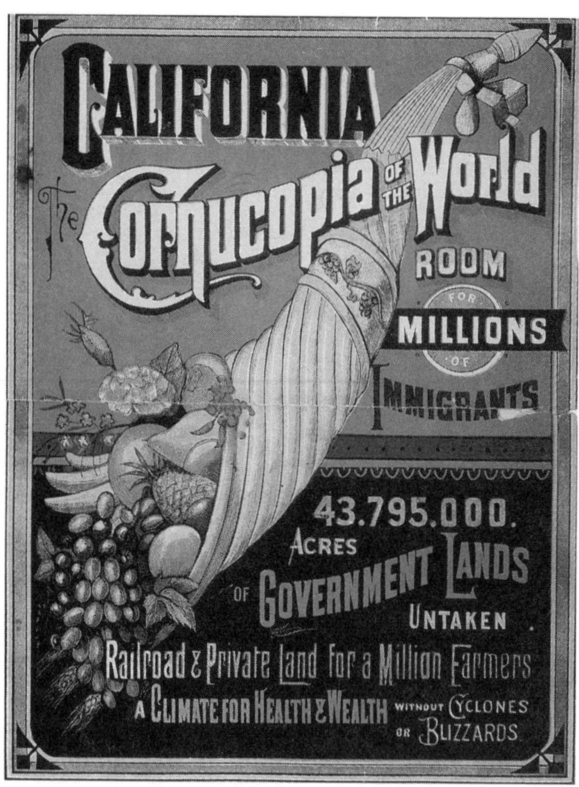

1. **Understanding Key Concepts** What does the booklet advertise? How many people does it claim California can support?
2. **Comparing** How do the population claims contradict California's arguments for restricting Chinese immigration that you read about in the case study?
3. **Making Inferences** What characteristics of the Chinese made them desirable as workers in California?

Case Study Review

Identifying Main Ideas

1. Why were Chinese immigrants recruited to help build the transcontinental railroad?
2. Why did white workers resent the Chinese?
3. How did the Chinese Exclusion Act affect Chinese immigrants?
4. Why did most Chinese immigrants live and work in Chinatowns in the late 1800s and early 1900s?

Working Together

Work with a partner to write a short one-act play about the Chinese attempt to strike for better working conditions on the railroads. Characters in the play might be Chinese workers and strike leaders, other railroad workers, railroad owners, and newspaper reporters. The Chinese workers should defend their reasons for wanting better pay and shorter work days.

Active Learning

Giving a Speech Review the notes you took while reading this case study. Imagine it is the year 2019. In a few weeks, the United States will celebrate the 150th anniversary of the completion of the transcontinental railroad. You have been asked to give a speech honoring the contributions and sacrifices of Chinese workers who helped build the railroad. First outline your speech, and then write a first draft. Revise your draft as necessary, and read your speech to the class.

Lessons for Today

The Chinese Six Companies worked hard to protect the rights of early Chinese immigrants. Think of another organization that looks out for the rights of its members today. What does this organization fight for? How does it help people improve their lives? Write a description of this organization and then explain your findings to the class.

What Might You Have Done?

Imagine that you belong to a union that calls for restrictions on immigration in order to protect wages. The union has greatly improved your working conditions, and you want to support it. However, you have many friends and relatives back home, and you would like for them to be able to join you in the United States. Immigration restrictions might hurt their chances of coming. Your union asks you to sign a petition against immigration. What would you do? Write a short response describing your choice and your feelings about it.

CRITICAL THINKING

Comparing Points of View on Immigration

Playing a Role

When you role-play, you play the part of another person. You try to think like that person and communicate that person's ideas. Role-playing can help you to understand someone else's point of view.

People often look at historical events from different points of view. People who feel strongly about an issue are often surprised to find out that a person on the opposite side of an issue feels just as strongly. One of the most difficult tasks for a critical thinker is to "try to put yourself in the other person's shoes"—to try to look at events from a different point of view.

Form groups of five. Have each person in the group role-play one of the following people from the late 1800s:

- a wealthy railroad company owner
- a Chinese immigrant laborer
- a California politician
- a white native-born American laborer
- a recent European immigrant

From the viewpoint of the role you are playing, think carefully about the following questions. Try to answer the questions as the person you are role-playing would answer them.

1. **Analysis** How do Chinese immigrants pose a threat to native-born laborers?
2. **Drawing Conclusions** What, if any, restrictions should there be on Chinese immigration?
3. **Forming an Opinion** Should Chinese immigrants living in the United States be entitled to the same rights as other foreign-born residents? Why or why not?

Discussion

As a group, have a discussion in which you present and compare your different points of view. Be sure everyone has a chance to speak. Continuing to play your respective roles, try to come to a compromise that will satisfy all persons involved.

This picture shows how an artist interpreted the trial of Italian immigrants Sacco and Vanzetti.

CASE STUDY 3

POLICIES AND PREJUDICE

CRITICAL QUESTIONS

- What factors led to the growth of prejudice against immigrants during the 1800s?
- What law is seen as the turning point in U.S. immigration policy?

TERMS TO KNOW

- anarchists
- nativists
- prejudice
- racism
- discrimination
- assimilate
- nationalism
- literacy test
- Red Scare
- quotas
- interned
- amnesty

ACTIVE LEARNING

After you read this case study, you will be asked to create a time line of immigration law that is based on information in the case study. As you read, take notes about important policies and dates. The Active Learning boxes will offer suggestions to help you complete your time line.

It was quiet on the night of August 23, 1927, despite the large crowd of people gathered in the open square outside Charlestown Prison in Boston, Massachusetts. The police, who were carrying pistols, hand grenades, and tear gas bombs, sat high on their horses watching the crowd and waiting for the first signs of unrest. The minutes ticked by, then the hours, as the people waited patiently, mournfully, for the stroke of midnight when the light in the prison tower would blink on and off.

These people were witnessing the climax of a story that began in the spring of 1920, when police charged Italian immigrants Nicola Sacco and Bartolomeo Vanzetti for the robbery and murder of a shoe factory paymaster and his guard. Both men had strong alibis, and the evidence against them was weak. Many felt Sacco and Vanzetti were being charged not because they were guilty but because of their Italian nationality and their political beliefs. Even the judge who tried the two men made comments against them and what they stood for.

Sacco and Vanzetti were **anarchists**, people who believe in a society without government or laws. Many Americans saw these beliefs as a threat to democracy; they feared that anarchists might plot to overthrow the U.S. government. These fears led to widespread anti-immigrant hysteria, especially against immigrants from Italy and other countries with strong anarchist or communist movements. Many people thought this hysteria greatly influenced the outcome of Sacco and Vanzetti's trial, which ended on July 14, 1921, with a verdict of guilty. The sentence—death.

People in countries all over the world protested the trial of Sacco and Vanzetti. Protesters in Switzerland attacked an American consulate; a strike in Paris shut down the entire city; and in the United States, people picketed, booed, shouted, and jeered as police officers broke up protest marches and arrested demonstrators.

Sacco and Vanzetti's lawyers and other supporters appealed their case for six years. They presented evidence that prosecution witnesses had lied, that police officers had acted illegally, and that a convicted bank robber had confessed to the crime. But in the end, it was no use.

On August 23, 1927, Sacco and Vanzetti were each strapped into an electric chair at Charlestown Prison and electrocuted at midnight. The large crowd of people waiting outside the prison slowly scattered into the night. Through their deaths, Sacco and Vanzetti became powerful symbols of social injustice and anti-immigrant prejudice.

Sacco and Vanzetti were found guilty, despite testimony that government officials brought the charges in order to deport them, evidence that a different gun may have been used during the crime, and a confession by a convicted murderer that he was responsible.

1 Nativism

As more and more immigrants arrived in the United States, the attitudes of native-born Americans toward immigration began to shift. Immigrants who came to the United States in the 1700s and during the early 1800s had been needed to develop farmland, populate new territories, build canals, and work in factories and mines. However, by the mid-1800s, the U.S. population had grown to over 13 million, and many immigrants were competing with native-born Americans for work.

Many native workers lost their jobs to immigrants, who accepted lower wages because they were desperate for work. Frustrated by employers who hired cheap foreign labor, native-born workers often directed their anger toward the immigrants, accusing them of stealing jobs and holding down wages.

Some people also blamed immigrants for the increasing poverty, crime, and disease that flourished in crowded cities and towns, and they pointed to the burden placed on charitable organizations in those two areas. They felt that the United States could not continue to absorb so many new arrivals; they wanted new laws to restrict immigration.

In 1854, one U.S. senator declared,

> *In the great cities of the Republic . . . the evils which have grown out of the admission of these...immigrants have become gigantic—frightful.*

People who felt strongly that U.S. laws should favor native-born Americans were called **nativists**. Nativists tried to convince Congress to pass laws restricting immigration. Many nativist ideas were based on practical concerns, such as job competition and increased crime. But they were also based on **prejudice**, a dislike of people who are different, and **racism**, the belief that one race is superior or inferior to another.

Nativists claimed that problems of poverty and crime were caused by character flaws in immigrants. However, the real causes included poor housing, low wages, and **discrimination**, or unfair treatment.

During the period from the late 1830s to mid-1850s, nativists, most of whom belonged to Protestant religions, directed their anger toward newly arrived Irish and German immigrants, most of whom were Catholic. Nativists resented Catholics because of their religious and political beliefs. They accused Catholics of being loyal to the Pope rather than to the United States. In eastern cities, such as Boston and New York City, anti-Catholic demonstrations sometimes became violent, resulting in riots and the burning of Catholic convents and churches.

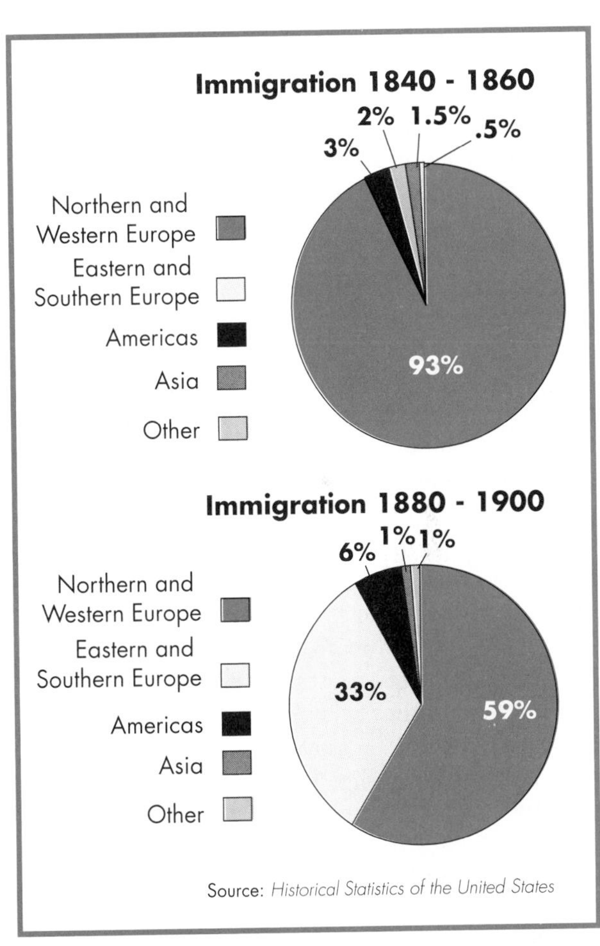

These circle graphs show how immigration patterns changed. From which areas of Europe did immigration increase? How might that change have affected nativist feelings?

No Irish Need Apply

Nativists especially resented Irish Catholic immigrants, whose numbers quickly grew into the hundreds of thousands due to a potato famine in Ireland. Most of the Irish who arrived in the 1850s, fleeing the potato famine, had little money and few skills.

Nativists wrote articles about the Irish, portraying them as lazy, uneducated, untrustworthy, and hard-drinking. These stereotypes led to widespread fear and discrimination that lasted well into the 1900s. "No Irish Need Apply" signs appeared frequently on storefronts and other places of business. As one Connecticut nativist declared,

> *I've never seen an Irishman whose word I could trust. If truth and a lie had equal value, he'd lie. They are tricky. They break the Ten Commandments every day, then go to a priest and it's all wiped out.*

The Know-Nothings

During the 1840s, nativists came together to form a new political party called the Know-Nothings, which was so named because its members were sworn to secrecy. When questioned about party activities, members would reply, "I know nothing."

The Whig and the Democratic parties both supported pro-immigration policies. They hoped to attract votes from first- and second-generation immigrants who, by then, outnumbered native-born Americans in many major cities. The Know-Nothings pledged to support only nativist candidates and never to support an immigrant or Catholic candidate. For over a decade, they pushed for restrictive immigration laws, including a 21-year waiting period for naturalization.

At first, the Know-Nothings attracted significant support. However, by the mid-1850s, the party had split over the question of slavery, which had become a major social and political issue. In addition, many people were joining the new Republican party. This political party, with such leaders as John C. Frémont and Abraham Lincoln, supported an antislavery platform. As a result, the Know-Nothing party lost members and soon died out. In 1864, the Republican party declared its support for immigration in the following statement:

> *Foreign immigration which in the past has added so much to the wealth, resources, and increase of power of this nation—the asylum of the oppressed of all nations—should be fostered and encouraged by a liberal and just policy.*

Nativism on the Rise

During the 1870s, the United States entered an economic depression. Businesses closed and many people lost their jobs. During that time, nativist voices once again began to rise as American workers competed with immigrants for available work. Accusing immigrants of holding down wages because they were willing to work for less money than native-born laborers, one nativist writer declared,

> *The influence upon the American rate of wages of a competition like this cannot fail to be [harmful] and even disastrous . . . Unless this access of vast numbers of unskilled workmen of the lowest type . . . shall be [stopped], it cannot fail to go on from bad to worse.*

Labor tensions often erupted in violence between native and immigrant workers, especially in California. There, thousands of Chinese immigrants had settled during the 1850s and 1860s when their labor was needed in mining and railroad construction. However, as those needs decreased and as fewer jobs became available, the Chinese increasingly competed for jobs with native-born whites. As a result, anti-Asian prejudice increased, and Chinese workers were often murdered, beaten, or run out of town. Recalls Gim Chang, a Chinatown resident in San Francisco,

> *I myself rarely left Chinatown. The area around Union Square was a dangerous place for us, you see, especially at nighttime. Chinese were often attacked by thugs there and all of us had to have a police whistle with us all the time.*

With unions, politicians, and anti-Asian sentiment on their side, nativists fought harder than ever for restrictions on immigration. Finally, in 1882, Congress passed the Chinese Exclusion

Some cartoonists ridiculed nativist ideas. In this cartoon, behind the nativists are the shadows of their immigrant ancestors. The cartoon shows that nativists themselves were descendants of immigrants.

Act, which barred the immigration of Chinese laborers and declared the Chinese "ineligible for citizenship." A turning point in immigration policy, the Chinese Exclusion Act was the first federal law to specifically limit immigration on the basis of race. Although some people claimed that the law was inspired by prejudice and that it legalized racial discrimination, few spoke out against it. In 1892, Congress extended this immigration law for 10 more years; then in 1902, Congress made it "permanent."

Growing Fears

By the close of the 19th century, increasing numbers of immigrants were arriving from countries in Southern and Eastern Europe. Among them were Italians, Greeks, and Slavs, who were seeking work, as well as Polish and Russian Jews who were escaping religious persecution. Their numbers totaled nearly 13 million between 1900 and 1914.

With the arrival of so many new immigrants, new nativist concerns and prejudices began to surface. These "new" immigrants spoke different languages and followed different customs than those previous immigrants who had come from countries in Northern and Western Europe. Because of these differences, nativists felt they would not be able to **assimilate**, or adapt to, the American way of life. They claimed that the new groups of immigrants were inferior and blamed them for rising unemployment, poverty, and violence. Madison Grant, a nativist describing these immigrants in his book, *The Passing of the Great Race*, wrote,

> *The new immigration . . . contained a large and increasing number of the weak, the broken and the mentally cripple. The whole tone of American life . . . has been [made inferior] by them.*

Most immigrants were unprepared for this negative reception in what they had viewed as the "land of opportunity." Cosma Tangora Sullivan, an Italian immigrant in 1905, recalled,

> *We sort of got ashamed of being Italians, because we were harassed so much after we got here. We didn't realize that things like that were going to happen. It was a shock to us. And that went on for years.*

While nativists persecuted the new immigrants, some groups stood up for them. For example, politicians in areas with growing numbers of naturalized citizens supported pro-immigration policies, hoping to win votes. The New Immigrants' Protective League, an organization that looked out for immigrant concerns, pointed out,

> *Those who are the loudest in their cry of "America for Americans" do not have to look very far back to find an ancestor who was an immigrant.*

The debate between nativists and pro-immigration forces continued over the next decade, but prejudice against immigrants became increasingly powerful. During World War I, American **nationalism**, or loyalty to one's country, swept the nation and strengthened anti-foreign feelings. In 1917, nativists won a major victory when Congress passed the Immigration Act. This law required all immigrants 16 years and older to read a 40-word passage in either English or "some other language or dialect, including Hebrew or Yiddish."

The Immigration Restriction League, based in Boston, had been pushing for a **literacy test** since 1894. Every time Congress passed a literacy test, the bills were vetoed by presidents. However, when President Woodrow Wilson vetoed the 1917 bill, congressional support was strong enough to override his veto. Nativists believed this literacy test would greatly reduce immigration from Southern and Eastern Europe.

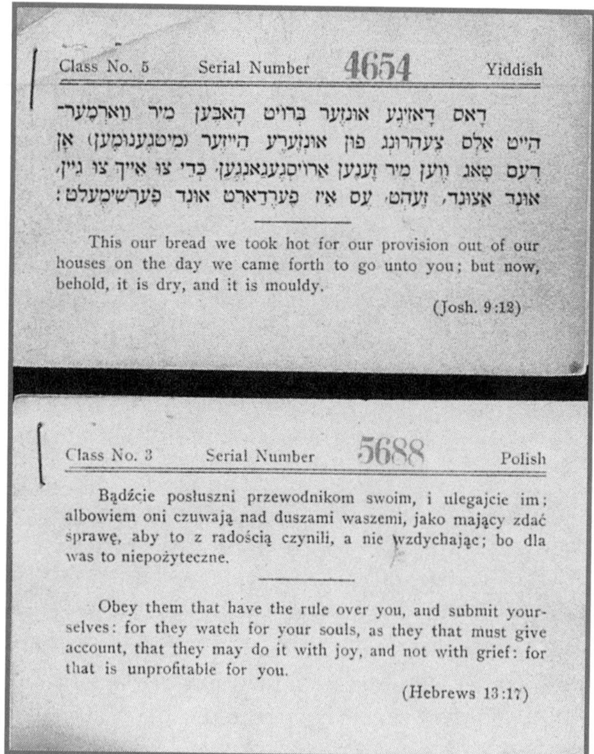

Class No. 5 Serial Number 4654 Yiddish

דאס דאזיגע אונזער ברויט האבען מיר ווארמער־
הייט אלס צעהרונג פון אונזערע הייזער (מיטגענומען) אן
דעם טאג ווען מיר זענען ארויסגעגאנגען, כדי צו אייך צו גיין,
אונד אצונד, זעהט, עס איז פערדארט אונד פערשימעלט:

This our bread we took hot for our provision out of our houses on the day we came forth to go unto you; but now, behold, it is dry, and it is mouldy.

(Josh. 9:12)

Class No. 3 Serial Number 5688 Polish

Bądźcie posłuszni przewodnikom swoim, i ulegajcie im; albowiem oni czuwają nad duszami waszemi, jako mający zdać sprawę, aby to z radością czynili, a nie wzdychając; bo dla was to niepożyteczne.

Obey them that have the rule over you, and submit yourselves: for they watch for your souls, as they that must give account, that they may do it with joy, and not with grief: for that is unprofitable for you.

(Hebrews 13:17)

The Immigration Act of 1917 required literacy tests—all immigrants over age 16 had to read a passage in their own language and in English.

Closing the Gates

The literacy test was not as effective as nativists had hoped. Most immigrants could read—or appeared to read—well enough to pass. In 1918, for example, the test had kept out fewer than 1,600 immigrants. By 1920, the population of the United States totaled 105 million, of which almost 14 million were foreign-born. Another 22 million had one or more foreign-born parents, bringing the entire immigrant family population to 36 million, or more than one-third of the total population.

Many Americans began to fear an "immigrant invasion." Some felt their American way of life was being threatened. Others feared that the new arrivals spread undemocratic ideas, such as anarchy and communism. Revolutions were occurring in some nations, such as Italy and Russia. Immigrants from those countries and other countries where rebellious movements were taking place, were considered suspicious. For example, Nicola Sacco and Bartolomeo Vanzetti, Italian immigrants and anarchists, were tried, convicted, and executed for murder on the basis of very little evidence.

The Sacco and Vanzetti case took place at the height of the anti-immigration hysteria of the 1920s, which was known as the **Red Scare**, and it was fueled by fears and prejudice against immigrants. Nativists used the Red Scare and the example of such "dangerous" immigrants as Sacco and Vanzetti to push for more effective restrictions on immigration. In response, Congress passed a temporary law in 1921 that set **quotas**, or limits, for immigration on the basis of recent population figures. While the law restricted overall immigration, it favored immigrants from Northern and Western Europe—immigrants from the same countries that had contributed to the population of the original 13 colonies. This law stopped total immigration at 350,000 people per year, and it sharply reduced immigration from Southern and Eastern Europe from an annual average of 783,000 to only 155,000.

In 1924, with the National Origins Act, Congress made the quota law permanent—and even stricter. It set an annual limit of 150,000 immigrants, and it based quotas on population figures from 1890. It also continued the exclusion of Asian immigrants. As a result, annual immigration from Southern and Eastern Europe dropped to below 25,000, and Asian immigration almost stopped. Congress later amended the law, basing quotas on population figures for 1920. Overall, the National Origins Act set the tone for immigration policy for the next 40 years.

Active Learning: Note some of the ways immigrants were treated as discussed in this section. List some of the policies and dates mentioned in this section for your time line. What are some of the major policy changes? Why are they important?

Thinking It Over

1. What immigrant groups did nativists oppose in the mid- to late 1800s?
2. **Making Comparisons** Why was the quota law more successful than the literacy law at restricting immigration?

In this cartoon, Uncle Sam checks immigrants as they enter the United States. Is the cartoon showing that the United States has an open door policy or a restrictive policy concerning immigration? How do you know?

2 A New Perspective

After the 1924 quota law went into effect, annual immigration dropped 50 percent, and over the next 20 years, economic depression and war reduced immigration even further. The Great Depression of 1929 was the worst in U.S. history. During the Great Depression, thousands of businesses folded, many banks closed, and millions of people lost their jobs and homes. The poor economy and lack of jobs reduced an already limited immigration to a trickle. In fact, from 1932 to 1935, the number of people leaving the United States was greater than the number of people entering.

In 1939, following on the heels of the Great Depression, World War II virtually shut down all immigration. Concerned about sabotage by immigrants who were suspected of having divided loyalties, Congress quickly passed the 1940 Alien Registration Act. This law required all resident aliens to register with the government.

The Second World War

In 1941, when the Japanese attacked Pearl Harbor, the United States joined the war against the Axis powers—Germany, Italy, and Japan. Almost immediately, German Americans, Italian Americans, and Japanese Americans faced discrimination from fellow citizens. But the Japanese were treated the worst.

Many people in the United States thought that Japanese Americans would be loyal to Japan and were part of a plan to destroy the United States, although there was never any evidence indicating this threat. Between 1942 and 1946, the U.S. government declared people of Japanese ancestry a threat to the safety of the United States. Without warning, the U.S. government ordered that all Japanese Americans would be rounded up. More than 120,000 Japanese Americans, two-thirds of them native-born citizens, were forced to take only what they could carry, to give up their jobs and homes, and to be **interned**, or held prisoner, in 10 isolated camps in the middle of the United States. Recalls Japanese American Yuri Kochiyama, a teenager during World War II,

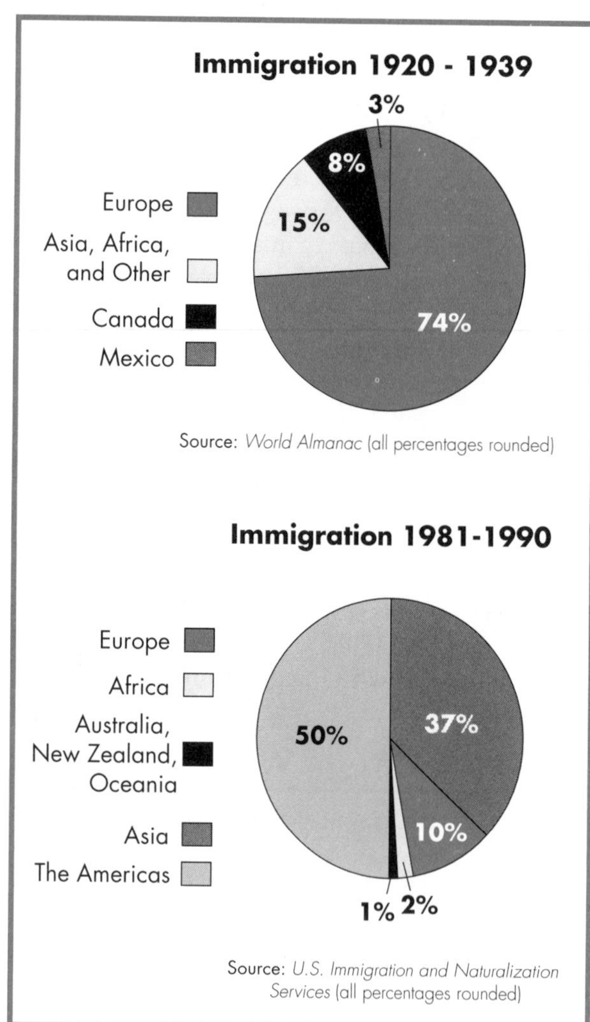

Patterns of immigration continue to change. Where do most recent immigrants come from?

> *Overnight, things changed for us. They took all the men who lived near the Pacific waters, and had anything to do with fishing. . . . They took those who were leaders of the community, or Japanese school teachers, or were teaching martial arts, or who were Buddhist priests. Those categories which would make them very 'Japanesey' were picked up.*

Chinese Americans, on the other hand, benefited greatly from the war. Having fought as allies with the United States, China won new respect. In 1943, as a gesture of appreciation, Congress repealed the 1882 Chinese Exclusion Act and gave the Chinese the right to citizenship. The gesture, however, was a token one, because the United States—still following the quota system—allowed only 100 Chinese immigrants to enter each year.

Relaxing the Laws

During World War II, the U.S. economy had recovered, helping to pull the country out of the ruins of the Great Depression. After the war, Americans anticipated a brighter future, and this anticipation, combined with reduced immigration over the previous 20 years, led to more relaxed attitudes about immigration.

In 1948, Congress passed the Displaced Persons Act of 1948, allowing 205,000 World War II refugees to enter the United States over two years. Four years later, it removed all remaining racial restrictions against immigration and naturalization with the Immigration and Nationality Act of 1952. This law came about largely because the United States hoped to stop the spread of communism in Eastern Europe and needed allies among people in Asia, Africa, and the Middle East. At the same time, due to anticommunist hysteria, the law strengthened the power of the U.S. government to deport undesirable aliens and required careful screening of new arrivals for possible membership in suspicious organizations.

The main purpose of the Immigration and Nationality Act, however, was to reunite families by allowing more relatives of naturalized citizens to enter as "non quota" immigrants. Families separated during years of restrictive quotas, depression, and war, could finally be brought together.

Active Learning: This section has some important dates that you will want to add to your time line. Review what significant changes were made to the quota laws and when the quota system was finally abolished.

A New System

Although the Immigration and Nationality Act of 1952 had relaxed naturalization laws, it still used national origins as a basis for how many newcomers could enter the United States, keeping the number of "undesirables" low. However, the Civil Rights movement of the 1950s and 1960s had made people more sensitive to issues of discrimination, and in 1965, Congress finally eliminated the national origin system of immigration, replacing it with a new system that tied admissions to factors such as family relationships, skills, and refugee status. The Immigration Act of 1965 allowed immigrants already in the United States to bring over their relatives, who in turn could bring over more relatives. This way of emigrating is called chain migration.

The Immigration Act of 1965 capped immigration at 290,000 and replaced quotas for individual countries with general quotas for the entire Eastern and Western hemispheres, ending discrimination against southeastern Europe, Asia, and the Pacific countries. The most drastic revision of immigration policy since the quota acts of the 1920s, the new law allowed freer acceptance of people from all parts of the world.

This new law, which continues to guide U.S. policy today, brought about a great increase in immigration, especially the chain migration of relatives. In 1978, amendments to the law replaced hemispheric quotas with a single worldwide quota.

Special Exceptions

During the 1970s, largely as a result of the Vietnam War, the United States recognized a need for special exceptions to immigration quotas to accommodate refugees. Earlier acts tried to include them as part

During World War II, the U.S. government questioned the loyalty of the Japanese in this country. They were rounded up and taken to guarded camps where they lived for the length of the war.

of existing quota and preference systems, but these efforts were not nearly enough.

Between 1975 and 1979, with about 400,000 Vietnamese and other Southeast Asian refugees flowing into the country, the need for new laws was finally realized. Lang Ngan, a Vietnamese refugee who came to the United States in 1975 during the first wave of evacuations, recalls her escape from Vietnam and her first few months in this country. She says,

> *There was no time to talk to friends or relatives because the evacuation was supposed to be secret, and we were not allowed to tell our relatives. We couldn't even take money out of the bank . . . In the beginning, I wanted to go back to Vietnam, because life was so different. Even the mailbox was different. Every evening, we opened it and it was full of papers and envelopes. I was afraid to throw away anything in case it was important, so I would read every word—thinking they were letters—not realizing this was advertising, junk.*

Congress responded to the refugee situation with the Refugee Act of 1980. This law removed refugees from the preference categories and established clear procedures for admission, allowing for both a regular flow and the emergency admission of refugees.

However, not all would-be refugees received equal treatment. Shortly after the Refugee Act went into effect, large numbers of Cubans and Haitians, both groups fleeing oppressive governments, came to the United States through southern Florida. The Cubans were initially welcomed, but most of the Haitians were turned away. Haitian activists and other critics were quick to point out that largely well-to-do "white" Cubans were accepted while mostly poor "black" Haitians were rejected. They wondered why this first major group of black refugees to the United States was being treated so differently from Cuban or Vietnamese or Russian refugees.

Thinking It Over

1. How did World War II affect immigrants living in the United States who came from countries the United States was fighting?
2. **Making Inferences** Why do you think Haitian immigrants were treated differently from other immigrants?

When the Vietnam War ended, many Vietnamese refugees came to the United States. By 1980, more than 200,000 Vietnamese were living in this country. Large numbers settled in California, Texas, and along the Gulf Coast.

A Good Book to Read

American Immigration: Should the Open Door Be Closed? by Gerald Leinwand. Franklin Watts, 1995.

This book puts the current immigration debate into historical perspective and offers numerous quotes and examples of how over the years each new wave of immigrants has been perceived as a "threat" to Americans.

3 Deciding Who Should Enter

During the 1970s, changing attitudes toward immigration and immigrants from particular countries continued. Immigration once again became a major social concern. For the first time since the 1920s, strong nativist attitudes resurfaced. Americans worried about the health of the U.S. economy, a severe oil shortage, and unsettling political events such as the Iranian hostage crisis, in which militant Iranians stormed the American Embassy in Tehran and held 50 Americans hostage for more than a year.

Moreover, 37 percent of all legal immigrants came from Asia and 47 percent came from Mexico, the Caribbean, and Latin America. Many Americans, concerned about decreasing immigration from Europe, once again debated issues of culture and assimilation. They questioned whether the United States could—or should—accommodate many more foreigners.

Evaluating Immigration

A 1981 report by a special U.S. government committee called the Select Commission on Immigration and Refugee Policy evaluated immigration policies and procedures and concluded that limiting immigration and controlling illegal immigration were in the national interest. It argued that the United States could not afford to set aside more than 20 percent of new jobs for foreign workers without doing "a disservice to our own poor and unfortunate."

Although many Americans agreed with these sentiments, many others did not. Some saw immigration as an opportunity for economic growth. A report by the Council of Economic Advisors stated:

> *There is evidence that immigration has increased job opportunities and wage levels for other workers . . . Immigrants come to this country seeking a better life, and their personal investments and hard work provide economic benefits to themselves and to the country as a whole.*

For five years, the debate continued in Congress and in the media. Finally, in 1986, with much controversy and many last-minute changes, Congress passed the Immigration Reform and Control Act. The new law consisted mainly of revisions to the existing policy, and legal immigration continued to grow throughout the 1980s. At the same time, the law attempted to control illegal immigration by requiring employers to verify the citizenship status of all newly hired employees and by fining employers who knowingly hired undocumented workers.

The law also allowed illegal aliens who had lived in the United States since at least 1981 to apply for **amnesty**, a program through which they could apply for U.S. citizenship as long as they showed proof of residency for the past five years. More than three million illegal aliens embraced the opportunity to become "legal." Alberto Solis, a Mexican immigrant who had lived in fear of deportation for 10 years before applying for amnesty under the new law, recalled,

> *I was able to work better. . . . when I was legal . . . I felt better, I could buy what I wanted: machinery, a new pick-up, anything I wanted. And without fear. Before, I was afraid to do anything, to buy anything, to plan.*

Still, many Hispanics were angry that aliens had to present proof of residency in order to qualify for amnesty. They criticized the law as being racist in its mistreatment of non-European refugees. William Tamayo, a critic of the new law, declared,

> *There is a reason the Statue of Liberty faces Europe and has its back to Asia and South America. We were never welcomed here.*

Ongoing Debates

The Immigration Act of 1990—still effective today—raised the annual limit on immigration to 675,000. This law also created separate categories for family-sponsored, employment-based, and "diversity" immigrants. In addition, it revised the grounds for exclusion and deportation, easing restrictions that had denied entrance to many people in the past.

By 1996, there were more than 24 million legal immigrants living in the United States, accounting for over 9 percent of the population, and millions more—both legal and illegal—continue to come. The United States is seeing its largest influx of immigrants since the turn of the century. More than half come from Mexico, the Philippines, Vietnam, the Dominican Republic, mainland China and Taiwan, Korea, and India.

The new wave of immigrants differs from previous waves. Many newcomers fall into one of two divisions. One group includes highly educated people. About 12 percent of these immigrants have advanced college degrees; in contrast, the total for native-born Americans is about 8 percent. The other group includes immigrants with little education. More than 33 percent of all immigrants have no high school diploma, which is double the rate for native-born citizens.

As more and more immigrants enter the country, state and local governments struggle to meet their needs for education, jobs, and health services. Although many midwestern cities have seen an increase in immigration populations, about 60 percent of all foreign-born residents live in a few big cities—Los Angeles, New York City, San Francisco, Chicago, Miami, Washington, D.C., and Houston. In some states, such as Florida, Texas, and California, debates rage about issues such as language and bilingual education. This is particularly true in states like California, where as many as 40 percent of the students speak little or no English. In Miami, three-fourths of the population speak a language other than English at home, and 67 percent say that they do not understand English. In New York City, 4 out of 10 residents speak a language other than English at home.

Proposition 187

One of the biggest ongoing debates involves whether government services to immigrants should be limited. Attempts in 1994 to implement Proposition 187, a California law denying medical and educational services to illegal immigrants, was met with forceful opposition. California students walked out of their public high schools and middle schools in protest. Many students, parents, educators, and community members rallied together. One newspaper editorial stated:

> *Proposition 187 . . . forces public officials to deny vital services to anyone they SUSPECT might not be a legal resident. But Proposition 187 doesn't define the basis for such suspicion. Is it the way you speak? The sound of your last name? The shade of your skin?*

In March 1998, U.S. District Judge Mariana Pfaelzer declared Proposition 187 unconstitutional, asserting that only the federal government, not the states, can regulate immigration. Says Tomas Saenz, counsel for the Mexican American Legal Defense and Educational Fund,

> *It vindicates the important constitutional principle that we cannot be one nation unless we have one immigration policy set by the federal government.*

The Welfare Reform Act

Likewise, the Welfare Reform Act of 1996 has met with controversy. Taking effect in late 1997, the Act called for cutbacks in Food Stamps and other federal benefits to immigrants, and it imposed a waiting period of 5 years from the date of entry before new immigrants are eligible to receive them at all. Since first announced, the Welfare Reform Act has been hotly debated. Some opponents of the law

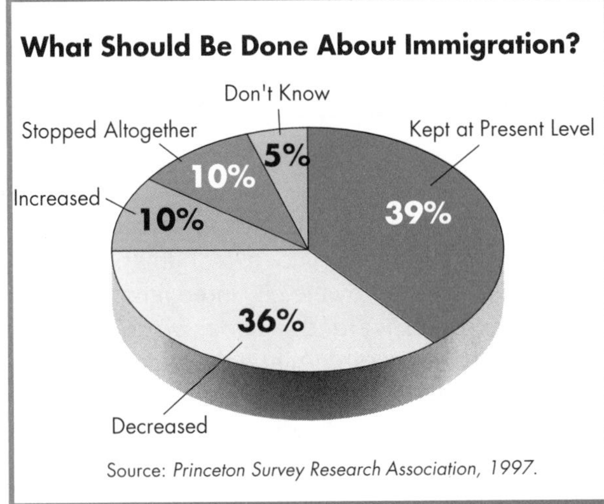

This graph shows how many people may feel about immigration. Which opinion do most people hold?

argue that it unfairly targets legal immigrants. About 6 percent of all immigrants receive some form of welfare, and this is double the rate for native-born Americans. Now many immigrants who had previously qualified for certain services will no longer be eligible to receive them and illegal immigrants, with rare exceptions, are not eligible for any benefits at all.

George Soros, a wealthy Hungarian immigrant who came to the United States in 1950, pledged $50 million to assist immigrants affected by welfare reform. Says Soros,

> *The Statue of Liberty embraces those 'yearning to breathe free,' but the current mean-spirited attack on immigrants threatens to choke them.*

Into the Future

Each new group of immigrants—from the early 1800s to the present—has faced prejudice and discrimination due to race, religion, political beliefs, or economic fears, and each has had to fight for its acceptance. Yet each new group, once assimilated, has imposed similar treatment on those who followed.

As Americans enter the 21st century, how future immigrants are viewed will depend on prevailing prejudices and social and economic concerns of the time. Many questions will be considered: Can the labor force accommodate more foreigners? Will immigrants take jobs from American workers? Will immigrants bring down wages? Increase crime? Overburden taxpayers? Will they threaten the "American" way of life? The questions will remain the same, and the answers are sure to vary.

The only thing that seems certain is that when the future looks promising, Americans are more likely to welcome foreigners to join in their prosperity. But when times are hard, prejudice once again rises to the surface, and the doors to the United States begin to close.

Thinking It Over

1. How did amnesty benefit illegal aliens?
2. **Making Inferences** Why do you think students and teachers reacted so strongly to Proposition 187?

GOING TO THE SOURCE

Bartolomeo Vanzetti's Final Statement

In 1997, on the seventieth anniversary of the death of Italian immigrants Nicola Sacco and Bartolomeo Vanzetti, Boston's first Italian-American mayor accepted a monument honoring the two men. The 7-foot sculpture, which had been rejected by the city three times in the past, shows Sacco and Vanzetti facing tilted scales of justice and includes words from Vanzetti's statement to the court on being sentenced to death. Although people continue to disagree as to whether the two men were innocent or guilty, most agree that they were treated unfairly because of their unpopular political beliefs. Below is Vanzetti's final statement. Read the statement and then answer the questions that follow.

> *"If it had not been for this, I might have lived out my life, talking at street corners to scorning men. I might have died unmarked, unknown, a failure. Now we are not a failure. This is our career and our triumph. Never in our full life can we do such work for tolerance, for justice, for man's understanding of man, as now we do by an accident. Our words—our lives—our pains—nothing! The taking of our lives—lives of a good shoemaker and a poor fish peddler—all!"*
>
> *—Bartolomeo Vanzetti,*
> *statement in court on*
> *being sentenced to death*

1. On what point do most people agree regarding Sacco and Vanzetti?
2. **Drawing Conclusions** To what is Vanzetti referring when he says, "This is our career and our triumph."?
3. **Making Inferences** Why do you think the city of Boston rejected the sculpture of Sacco and Vanzetti in the past?

Case Study Review

Identifying Main Ideas

1. What is nativism, and what immigration policies did it bring about in the late 1800s and early 1900s?
2. How did the National Origins Act of 1924 affect immigration?
3. How and why did attitudes toward immigration change during the 1960s?
4. What are some factors that encourage Americans to welcome or bar immigrants?

Working Together

Form a small group of four or six students. Discuss the reasons why people favor restrictions on immigration and the reasons they oppose restrictions. Then organize a debate, with half of each small group taking one side of the issue and half taking the other side. At the close of the debate, try to come up with policy suggestions that both sides agree on.

Active Learning

Make a Time Line Review the notes you took while reading this case study. Use your notes to create a time line of immigration policy and law from the mid-1800s through 1996. Then, using library and media sources, research any recent changes in immigration law and include them on your time line. Illustrate your time line with pictures that you have drawn or cut from magazines and newspapers.

Lessons for Today

As you have read, recent changes in immigration policy have been highly controversial. Use library and media resources to research the different points of view on the Welfare Reform Act as it pertains to immigration. What immigrants are affected by the law and how? Do you think the law is an effective way to control immigration? Why or why not? Write a brief essay explaining your opinion.

What Might You Have Done?

Imagine that you are a police officer investigating the case against Sacco and Vanzetti. You discover that some of your fellow officers are withholding important evidence that could affect the outcome of the trial. You know that your superiors, the judge, and many local politicians are determined to see the men convicted, so speaking up about what you know would probably have little effect and could cost you your job. What would you do and why?

CRITICAL THINKING

Understanding Cause and Effect

Identifying Key Words

Certain words can help you identify causes and effects. When analyzing a passage, the following words may indicate a cause:

because
due to
since

The following words may indicate an effect:

as a result
consequently
therefore

Causes are incidents or conditions that produce an effect. They explain why the effect happened. Effects are incidents or conditions that the cause brings about. They explain what happened as a result of the causes. Over the years, changes in U.S. immigration policy have been influenced by many conditions, and each change brought about its own set of—sometimes predictable, sometimes surprising—results. In other words, each new law had both causes and effects.

Use the graphic organizer below to review one cause and one effect of the 1882 Chinese Exclusion Act. Then read the list of immigration laws that follow. In your notebook, write at least one cause or one effect for each law.

CAUSE	LAW	EFFECT
Thousands of Chinese immigrants are competing with white workers for jobs.	Congress passes a law that restricts Chinese immigration.	Discrimination against Chinese immigrants increases and often becomes violent.

Laws

1. Congress passes a literacy test to restrict immigration.
2. In 1924, a new quota law sets limits on immigration on the basis of population figures for 1890.
3. Proposition 187 denies medical and educational services to illegal immigrants in California.
4. The Welfare Reform Act of 1996 cuts benefits to legal immigrants.

In the early 1900s, these women arrived at the Ellis Island immigration station from the West Indies.

CASE STUDY 4

IMMIGRANTS SEARCH FOR OPPORTUNITY

CRITICAL QUESTIONS

- What were the differences in education and politics between West Indians and African Americans, and how did those differences lead to tension?
- How did the fact that West Indians came from areas in which they were a majority of the population affect their attitudes in the United States where they became a minority?

TERMS TO KNOW

- emigrated
- migrated
- West Indian
- Harlem Renaissance
- mulattos

ACTIVE LEARNING

Imagine that you are a new immigrant from the West Indies who has come to Harlem in the 1920s. You have to find work and make enough money to pay for your rent and food, as well as save some money to send home. In this exercise, you will write journal entries about your observations and experiences. Look for the Active Learning boxes. They will offer tips for making your entries more realistic.

On the evening of August 2, 1920, an excited crowd of more than 25,000 people jammed into Madison Square Garden in New York City. Most had come from Harlem, the area of New York City north of 133rd Street in Manhattan, which was then a vibrant community of African American businesses, newspapers, hotels, and churches.

Some of the people in the crowd were African Americans who had come North as part of the Great Migration during World War I. Others were among the thousands of immigrants who had **emigrated** from the West Indies to New York City during the previous two decades. Emigrate means to leave one's native country to settle elsewhere.

The crowd was gathered for the convention of the Universal Negro Improvement Association (U.N.I.A.), one of the largest organizations of its time. The people had assembled to hear the president and founder of the U.N.I.A. This man had himself emigrated to the United States from Jamaica in 1916. His name was Marcus Garvey, and on that evening in 1920, he was perhaps the most famous person in this thriving African American and West Indian culture.

The crowd roared as Garvey walked to the podium. They grew silent as he addressed them. He said,

> *The Negroes of the world . . . are striking back towards Africa to make her the big black republic. The barrier is the white man who now dominates Africa. . . . it is to his interest to clear out of Africa now, because we are coming 400,000,000 strong and we mean to retake every square inch of African territory belonging to us by right Divine. . . . We are out to get what has belonged to us politically, socially, economically, and in every way.*

Active Learning: You are in the crowd that has just heard Marcus Garvey speak. Describe the experience as you begin to write your journal entries. What part of Garvey's message appealed to you? What about his message did not appeal to you?

1 The Way North

The term **West Indian** refers to people from English-speaking islands in the Caribbean, generally those islands that had been colonies of Great Britain. By the late 1800s, the population of the West Indies was made up of three groups. White people were the upper class. They were also the smallest group, but they owned most of the land.

Because the number of whites was low, there was a need for people to serve as merchants, teachers, civil servants—and in other roles. This was the middle class, and it was largely made up of **mulattos**—people of mixed white and African ancestry.

The middle class emerged because the British rulers recognized that their colonies in the West Indies would fail without an educated force of workers and civil servants to run them. For that reason, local inhabitants were educated and trained to police the streets, to run the schools, and to serve in government offices.

The need to have an educated population meant that almost all West Indians could read and write English. The literacy rate for West Indians was more than 90 percent—one of the highest at that time of any place in the world.

The vast majority of the population made up the lower class. These people were the descendants of African slaves. Most worked on plantations or farmed their own small plots of land. Others left the poverty of the countryside for work in nearby towns. Those who found jobs there labored in filthy, dangerous conditions for low wages.

'Panama Money'

Between 1896 and 1936, the population of the West Indies grew by 50 percent. As the population continued to grow, opportunities became fewer and fewer. As was the case with most waves of immigration, a large number of people left their homelands searching for better lives.

Many thousands of West Indians emigrated to the new nation of Panama in Central America. The reason was the Panama Canal. The "Big Ditch," as it was called, was being built across the Isthmus of Panama to shorten the distance between the Atlantic and the Pacific oceans. Between the mid-1880s and 1914, more than 100,000 West Indians **migrated,** or moved, to Panama to help build the canal.

So many West Indians migrated to Panama during the late 19th and early 20th century that the term "Panama Money" became part of the language on the islands. The term referred to cash that enabled workers who returned to Jamaica, Barbados, or elsewhere in the West Indies to pay for their passages to the United States.

When the Panama Canal opened in 1914, these West Indians were left without jobs. Many chose to migrate to other Caribbean countries, such as Cuba or the Dominican Republic. In those countries the United Fruit Company had purchased huge areas of land to grow bananas, a fruit that had recently attained popularity in the United States. Soon the "Banana Boats" that were steaming northward carrying fruit were also carrying West Indians who worked for United Fruit and who decided to emigrate to the United States.

World War I and Immigration

Besides being the year the Panama Canal opened, 1914 marked the beginning of World War I in Europe. The war would continue for 4 years, and it just about stopped immigration to the United States from the countries of Europe.

As the war continued in Europe, allies of the United States, such as England and France,

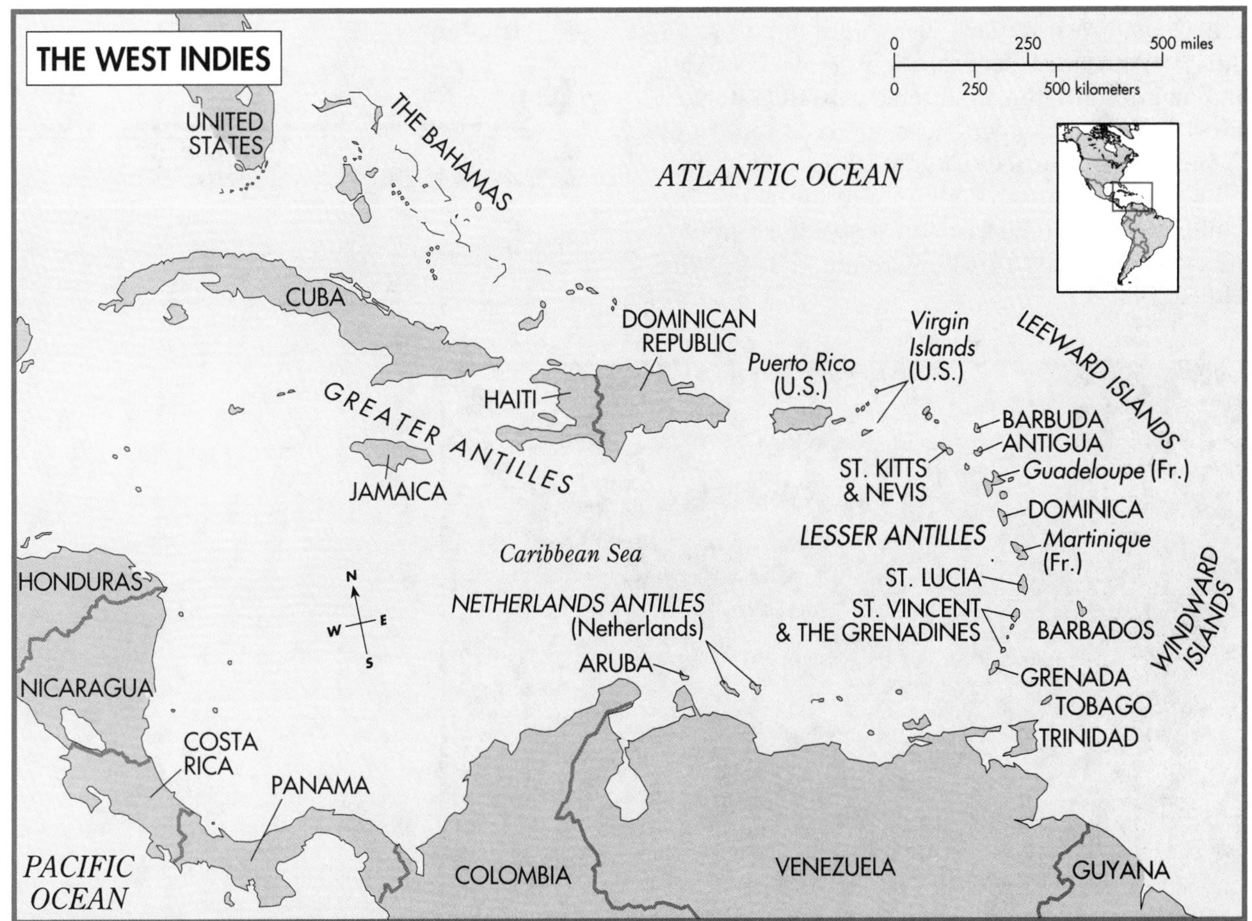

The West Indies, as a chain of islands, stretch 2,000 miles from near the tip of Florida to the coast of Venezuela. Locate Cuba, Jamaica, Puerto Rico, and Trinidad.

required military supplies, food, and clothing. Many of those goods were produced in New York. Thus, the number of relatively well-paying factory jobs rose in the New York area. Because there were almost no European immigrants to fill the jobs, factory owners turned to other labor sources.

One source was the South. The wave of African Americans from the South occurred at the same time as the wave of West Indian emigration to New York City. However, despite the fact that both groups traced their roots to Africa, there were great differences between them.

Because of prejudice and segregation in the South, Southern African Americans were mostly uneducated and unskilled. By contrast, most West Indian immigrants could read and write English. More than 70 percent of these immigrants were either professional people, office workers, or skilled laborers. The advantage in education and in skills meant that West Indians were often hired before African Americans for many jobs. However, West Indian immigrants also suffered a disadvantage—most had never experienced the cold reality of American prejudice. Despite these problems, however, West Indians continued to stream into the United States. In the first 30 years of this century, more than 150,000 West Indians emigrated to the United States.

Why Harlem?

In the 1920s, Harlem, an area of New York City, became "The Promised Land" for many African Americans. They believed that traveling to Harlem would provide them the opportunity to own property and escape the brutal conditions under which they lived in the South. Harlem became the center of African American culture in the United States. Harlem was also a magnet for people from the West Indies.

Although New York City was not as brutally racist as cities in the South, in many ways it was just as segregated. Landlords refused to rent apartment to people of color in white neighborhoods. Many businesses refused to serve African Americans. Jobs for black workers, whether West Indian or African American, were often limited to the lowest-paying, most demeaning, and most dangerous.

Active Learning: Write some ideas for your journal entries describing your reaction to prejudice in the United States.

This photo shows a Jamaican marketplace in about 1915, when many immigrants began coming to the United States from the West Indies.

Thinking It Over

1. How did the opening of the Panama Canal and the outbreak of World War I affect emigration to the United States?
2. **Drawing Conclusions** What common problems might African Americans and West Indians have had in trying to adjust to life in the North?

2 Contributing to the Harlem Renaissance

When World War I ended, immigration increased from 141,000 people in 1919 to more than 800,000 by 1921. Because many Americans felt that their way of life was being threatened by immigrants, Congress passed immigration laws based on quotas. The quota law limited the number of people allowed into the United States from countries in Southern and Eastern Europe. In 1924, the National Origins Act limited immigration even more. The only countries that these laws did not affect were in the Western Hemisphere.

The effect of these laws allowed West Indian immigrants to enter the United States almost unrestricted through the 1920s. In addition, because the white immigrants with whom they might have competed for jobs were barred from entering, West Indians found many opportunities for employment. The great wave of West Indians arrived in Harlem.

A Rebirth of the Arts

In Harlem, music and the arts flourished. Many poems, novels, and plays concerned racial injustice and the struggle for equality.

This exciting time came to be known as the **Harlem Renaissance**—a rebirth of artistic activity. The Harlem Renaissance occurred at a time when African Americans created music, art, literature, and entertainment that was both culturally unique and also led to some of the finest artistic achievements in American history. Much of the Renaissance resulted because of the efforts of West Indian immigrants who were arriving in Harlem in growing numbers.

Writers' Voices

In 1925, *Opportunity*, an African American magazine, announced a literary contest. Among the winners was Claude McKay, a young writer from Jamaica. McKay became probably the best known West Indian writer during the Harlem Renaissance.

McKay had emigrated to the United States in 1912 to attend college, and he had moved to New York City. After McKay took a job as a railroad dining-car waiter, he traveled around the country. During 1919, many race riots exploded in U.S. cities where African American migrants had settled. As

Claude McKay worked as a longshoreman on the docks and as a waiter on the Pennsylvania Railroad. In his spare time, he wrote poems.

he traveled, McKay didn't stray far from the other workers, mostly African Americans, at stopovers in Washington, D.C. and Pittsburgh. He noted that when they walked from the trains to their boardinghouses, they often had to carry weapons for protection. The closeness he felt for fellow workers and his sympathy for the African Americans' struggle against prejudice influenced his writing.

McKay is best known as a poet. Among his many poems that reveal racial anger is "If We Must Die," a poem he wrote when race riots led to the deaths of many African Americans. The closing lines of the poem state McKay's feelings that dignity and courage are the weapons that African Americans need to fight for justice. He wrote,

What though before us lie the open grave?
Like men we'll face the murderous,
cowardly pack,
Pressed to the wall, dying, but fighting back!

McKay was not the only West Indian writer during this time. George Reginald Margetson, who came from the island of St. Kitts, wrote *The Fledgling Bard* and *Poetry Society*. His poetry focused on racial problems. Eulalie Spence, a playwright, was born on the island of Nevis. The characters in her plays, workers and churchgoers, were independent females. Amy Ashwood Garvey, who was from Jamaica and was Marcus Garvey's wife, wrote musical comedies. Eric Walrond, a native of New Guinea who was an editor for African American newspapers, wrote *Tropic Death*, a collection of short stories that focused on poor people in the West Indies and their experiences working in Panama.

Thinking It Over

1. What were the main ideas that Harlem Renaissance writers expressed in their work?
2. **Drawing Conclusions** How did the fact that McKay was a West Indian immigrant help fuel the anger in his writing?

3 The U.N.I.A. and Black Hopes

It was onto this scene of expectation, resentment, and rebirth that Marcus Garvey carried his message. By founding the U.N.I.A., Garvey's aim was "uniting all the Negro people of the world into one great body to establish a country and government all their own."

Although Garvey's goal was to take back Africa from the Europeans who had colonized it, he had more short-term goals as well. He dreamed of bringing a sense of pride and racial unity to all the people who traced their roots to Africa.

Garvey opened a chain of grocery stores and several other businesses, including restaurants, a printing plant, and a laundry. In 1919, he founded the Black Star Line, a steamship company. He intended to use both the shipping company and its profits to establish his African nations. Garvey sold shares in the Black Star Line to U.N.I.A. members.

Unfortunately, his group purchased a ship that was barely seaworthy. In addition, there were legal problems over the ship's ownership, and on its first voyage, a strike in Cuba prevented delivery of the ship's cargo.

Garvey Becomes a Hero

In the 1920s, Garvey became a hero throughout the black community. His U.N.I.A. promised everything that migrants and immigrants hoped to gain from their move to the North. At the height of the U.N.I.A. movement, Garvey claimed 4 million members, although a more conservative estimate of 500,000 is considered more accurate.

Garvey took a militant approach to dealing with white society. He avoided attachment to white political leaders and refused any financial support from white sources. This attitude outraged many African American leaders as well as powerful white groups.

Garvey's Downfall

In the early 1920s, Garvey set off on a path that led to his downfall as an African American leader.

Opposed to integration of any kind, Garvey approached an unusual source in his efforts to achieve complete segregation—the Ku Klux Klan. Other African American leaders considered this a disastrous alliance and asked the U.S. Attorney General to investigate the U.N.I.A.

In 1922, Garvey was charged with mail fraud for his financial dealings in his efforts to raise money for his shipping line. Though evidence against him was questionable, Garvey was sentenced to 5 years in prison, and upon release from prison, he was deported to his homeland.

Active Learning: Write your thoughts about the importance of the U.N.I.A. and how you feel about the way it ended.

Thinking It Over

1. What led to Garvey's downfall?
2. **Making Inferences** Besides Garvey's alliance with the Ku Klux Klan, what might have been some reasons that other African American leaders did not support him?

4 Working for the Dream

By the time Marcus Garvey was freed from prison and returned to Jamaica in the late 1920s, the flow of West Indian immigrants to the United States had slowed. The Great Depression of the late 1920s and 1930s had caused jobs to disappear almost overnight. Banks failed, factories closed, and millions of people lost their jobs.

During the 1930s, there was little reason for West Indians to migrate to the United States. Along with economic uncertainty, immigration laws permitted fewer than 1,000 immigrants from the West Indies to enter the United States each year.

Free to Emigrate

It was only at the end of the 1960s that West Indians were again free to emigrate to the United States in large numbers. Today, more than a million and a half West Indians live in the United States, mainly in New York City and places on the East Coast. Large West Indian communities also exist in California, Michigan, Illinois, and Florida.

For new immigrants, as had been the case in the past, the United States—for all of its problems—is a beacon of opportunity. But West Indian immigrants still face the traditional problems of all immigrants—how much of the homeland to leave behind and how much to bring along.

West Indians Celebrate

On each Labor Day in New York City, the streets come alive in the borough of Brooklyn. Eastern Parkway, a large highway, is closed to traffic for the day. Brightly-colored floats filled with West Indian calypso musicians parade in front of thousands. The smell of barbecued meat—the term, *barbeque,* is originally from the West Indies—fills the air. It is Carnival Day, a time for people who come from the West Indies to celebrate their culture. It is a time to honor people who are recent immigrants or whose parents and grandparents came from Jamaica, Trinidad, Nassau, St. Vincent, Grenada, Antigua, Barbados, and dozens of other places in the West Indies.

Thinking It Over

1. Why did fewer immigrants come to the United States during the Great Depression?
2. **Drawing Conclusions** Why might immigrants have a problem in balancing the culture of their homelands with the culture of the United States?

GOING TO THE SOURCE

Watching a U.N.I.A. Parade

Photographs often provide clues to the past and a feel for the time. They give us a clear idea of how people and places in recent history looked. The picture below shows a crowd watching a U.N.I.A. parade in Harlem in 1920. Study the picture and then answer the questions.

1. **Interpreting a Photograph** What are some differences in this photograph taken in 1920 and one that might be taken of a parade today?
2. **Drawing Conclusions** How would you feel being a member of the crowd?
3. **Making Inferences** What might have been the impact of this picture when it appeared in newspapers? What do you think was the impact of this picture when people outside the United States saw it?

Case Study Review

Identifying Main Ideas

1. Why were West Indian immigrants well educated?
2. How did the migration of people from the West Indies to Panama affect the later immigrations to the United States?
3. How did the tensions between African Americans and West Indians arise?

Working Together

Form a group with three or four classmates. Review this case study and choose one event that your group would like to write about for *Negro World.* Choose a controversial subject that the paper might take a stand on. Write a headline to go with the article or editorial. Use your school, local library, or the Internet for additional resources.

Active Learning

Writing a Journal Entry Review and revise the entries you wrote while reading the case study. Now write a final entry that summarizes the successes of West Indian immigrants in the United States.

Lessons for Today

Although West Indian immigrants and African Americans both trace their roots to Africa, a tension and dislike arose between the groups at certain times during the wave of West Indian immigration. Part of that tension was because West Indians, being better educated, were often chosen for jobs instead of African Americans. How might the opportunities people encounter change with their levels of education? Write a brief essay explaining your point of view on the importance of education.

What Might You Have Done?

It is 1920, and you are a recent West Indian immigrant and a follower of Marcus Garvey. When Garvey speaks of returning to Africa, most of your family agrees that the only way to find true equality is for people of color to return to Africa. You agree with Garvey's point of view, but you have just arrived in the United States and you have a place to live and a job. What might you do and why?

CRITICAL THINKING

Analyzing a Primary Source

Using First-hand Information

Historians use primary sources to learn about the past. A primary source gives first-hand information about people and events. Primary sources include letters, diaries, political documents, and newspaper editorials. Personal memoirs, paintings, photographs, and editorial cartoons are also primary sources.

The following primary source is a newspaper article that appeared in the New York *Herald Tribune* on August 5, 1926. The article describes the parade that opened that year's U.N.I.A. convention. Read the article and answer the questions that follow.

> *From every window on the route and from hot roof tops hung thousands of Negroes cheering the name of Marcus Garvey. . . . On the sidewalks ten deep stood 100,000 more waving and shouting and applauding as the procession opening the first day of the convention of UNIA went blaring by. But Marcus Garvey himself, dreamer of dreams for the future of the Negro race, was not present. He is in the Federal penitentiary in Atlanta, serving a term of five years for fraudulent use of the mails, but his grip on the Negroes of Harlem, whose new and conscious pride of race he was foremost in instilling, apparently has been weakened not at all by his absence.*

1. **Understanding Text** Why was Marcus Garvey absent from the parade?
2. **Understanding Key Concepts** According to the article, why was Garvey so popular with Harlem residents?
3. **Analyzing** Read again the information on pages that explains why Marcus Garvey was sentenced to prison. From the description of the crowd, what do you think their feelings about Garvey's crime might be? Explain.
4. **Synthesizing** Reread the quote on page 56 and the article on this page. Then form your own opinion about Garvey. Explain your opinion and give reasons to support it.

In the 1860s, many Irish workers helped build the Union Pacific Railroad that linked with the Central Pacific Railroad to form the first transcontinental railroad.

CASE STUDY 5

A NEW FORCE IN POLITICS

CRITICAL QUESTIONS

- What advantages enabled Irish immigrants to gain political power?
- How did the political machines of the 1800s affect conditions in Irish communities?

TERMS TO KNOW

- landlords
- cooper
- cholera
- confiscated
- Penal Laws
- Great Famine
- indentured servants
- shantytowns
- machines
- bosses

ACTIVE LEARNING

In this case study, you will read about why many Irish immigrants came to the United States in the 19th century and what they experienced after they arrived. At the end of the case study, you will be asked to write a newspaper article about Irish American struggles and triumphs. Use the suggestions in the Active Learning boxes to help you prepare your assignment.

Twenty-six-year old Patrick Joseph Kennedy had experienced more hardship than many men twice his age in Ireland. The son of poor farmers, oppressed and exploited by British **landlords**, or property owners, Patrick had seen his family and his friends struggle year after year to feed themselves on what little food they could raise, giving over the best of their crops as payment for rent.

Patrick was used to this harsh life; it was all he knew. But never had he seen anything so devastating as the deadly hunger that had gripped Ireland since 1846. That was when potatoes—the one crop that Irish farm families depended on most as food—had failed. As a fungus continually attacked growing plants, the potato crop failed year after year for 10 miserable years.

Hundreds of thousands of people died of starvation and disease. Ireland became a mass burial ground. In 1849, the worst year of the famine, Patrick grasped at his last chance for survival and made the difficult decision to leave his country. In search of new hope and opportunity, he boarded a ship bound for the United States.

During the 3,000-mile journey, Patrick met Bridget Murphy, a 24-year-old Irish woman also fleeing the famine. Romance blossomed, and Bridget and Patrick married shortly after their ship's arrival in Boston, Massachusetts.

Penniless, the Kennedys settled in a crowded East Boston ghetto. Patrick became a **cooper**, or barrel maker, in order to support his growing family. Their world was one of poverty, disease, and danger. In fact, shortly after they arrived, **cholera**, a fatal illness, swept through the Boston slums, killing more than 500 Irish immigrants and their children. In October 1858, after their last child, Patrick, Jr., was born, Patrick himself came down with cholera and died, leaving Bridget to support their four children on her own.

With the help of the Irish community, Bridget worked hard to raise her family. Her son, Patrick, Jr., thrived and eventually escaped the world of poverty that had killed his father. He earned enough money to open a restaurant and soon ventured into politics—beginning a legacy that would profoundly affect his parents' adopted country in years to come.

A Good Movie to See

The Irish in America. The History Channel, 1998 (100 minutes)

Narrated by Aidan Quinn, this two-cassette documentary presents highlights from the Irish immigrant experience through dramatic recreations of significant events, readings, songs, and interviews with historians.

1 Prisoners on Their Own Land

Ireland had been dominated by the British since 1171, when British troops, led by King Henry II of England, conquered the land. At that time, the British **confiscated**, or took away, Irish-owned lands and passed laws that limited Irish rights.

The British, who were primarily Protestant, controlled the Irish with these and other strict laws, known as **Penal Laws**. These laws were specifically aimed at Irish Catholics—who made up 80 percent of Ireland's population. Among other things, the Penal Laws banned Irish Catholics from voting, owning land, working in government, serving on a jury, studying at a university, carrying guns, and speaking Gaelic, their native language. These laws also barred them from almost every profession, including teaching.

Irish Catholics who broke the Penal Laws were fined, imprisoned, whipped, or sentenced to death. The British hoped that the laws would force Irish Catholics to convert to the Protestant religion.

Farming was one of the few jobs available to Irish Catholics; they lived on and farmed British plantations. Most of the crops they grew were used to pay the rent. Their single-room shacks consisted of mud walls, a dirt floor, and little or no furniture.

Patrick Kennedy came to the United States during the Great Famine. He started a family that has become an American legend.

A pile of straw served as a bed for an entire family—often as many as 15 people.

The Penal Laws were abolished by 1829. But by then, Irish Catholics had become trapped in a cycle of poverty from which there was virtually no escape.

Depending on Potatoes

English landlords owned 95 percent of the land in Ireland, and they demanded high rents and taxes. Irish farmers had to sell the corn, wheat, barley, and oats they grew to pay their rents. Almost all they grew on their farms was either sold or exported to Britain.

Irish farmers lived simple lives. Their diet consisted of oatmeal, milk, honey, butter, and potatoes—their most dependable crop. The potato had fed the Irish for generations; potatoes were rich in nutrients and easy to grow. A single family could eat up to 50 pounds of potatoes per day. Farmers harvested the potato crop in autumn and then buried potatoes in mounds of dirt and peat where they stayed fresh all year.

However, even growing enough potatoes to feed the Irish population soon became difficult. Between 1780 and 1841, the Irish population increased from 4.5 million to 8.2 million. Because Irish Catholic farmers were forced by law to divide their land between their sons, plots of land became smaller and smaller. Families were large, and farms that had originally fed one family now had to feed as many as ten. Before long, the farms became too small to divide. One farm, home to a single family in 1793, had 96 tenants by 1847.

With a good crop, a few acres of potatoes could feed a family of six for a year. However, with a poor crop—or a large family—the potatoes ran out well before the autumn harvest. When potato supplies ran low, families ate only one skimpy meal a day—and sometimes they starved.

The Potato Famine

In 1845, the situation took a disastrous turn. Throughout Ireland, a quick-growing fungus invaded the potato crop—the leaves turned black and the vegetable became slimy and inedible. Overnight, entire fields of potatoes rotted

Known as the **Great Famine**, or hunger, the potato rot continued for 10 years. As potato crops failed, three million poor Irish farmers struggled in vain to feed their families. They searched desperately through fields for berries, weeds, and leaves. They ate grass and gathered seaweed from the ocean. Many children died of starvation. A visitor, traveling through the land, recalled,

> *little children leaning against a fence—for they could not stand—their limbs fleshless, their bodies half naked, their faces of a pale greenish hue—children, who would never, it was too plain, grow up to be men and women.*

British landlords offered little help. They blamed the Irish for their problems, depicting them as drunkards and beggars. Some even suggested that the famine was a punishment because the Irish refused to give up their Catholic religion. Cruel landlords evicted families who were unable to pay their rent, leaving them to die homeless.

Eventually, the British were forced to take action. They set up soup kitchens and public work programs that enabled some families to receive food. But their efforts were half-hearted and not nearly enough. Most British simply didn't care whether the Irish lived or died. In fact, while millions of Irish starved to death, British landlords shipped thousands of tons of meat, grain, and cattle from Ireland to England. According to a British journalist, in a single day—November 18, 1848—landlords shipped out

> *47 bales of bacon, 120 casks and 135 barrels of pork, 5 casks of ham, 300 bags of flour, 300 head of cattle, 239 sheep, and 542 boxes of eggs.*

Farmers had to pay their rent every 6 months. Failure to pay resulted in being sent to jail or being evicted, and the homes were then burned. Because the Irish had no potato crop that they could use to pay their rent, landlords evicted hundreds of thousands of them from their homes. Many people died of starvation or went to live in workhouses—buildings where people with absolutely no money went to live. Workhouses were crowded; one workhouse in Limerick had 2,513 people crowded into space meant for 800 people. The workhouses were also full of disease. In the workhouses, the Irish were forced to wear prison uniforms and to eat porridge, an oatmeal soup, dished out from huge pots.

As the famine continued, the British still demanded that the starving Irish pay their rent and taxes. As almost all food was exported, food became scarce, and the price became so high that not many poor farmers could afford to buy what was available.

A Matter of Survival

During the famine years, it was clear that the Irish would never receive enough help from the British, so, like Patrick Kennedy, many took what they saw as their only course of action. They left their beloved homeland, believing that they would be better able to survive in the United States.

Although desperately poor, many found ways to make the transatlantic journey. Some hired themselves out as **indentured servants**, people who agreed to work for a certain number of years to pay off the cost of their passage. Some relied on money sent by family members already living in the United States. More often, however, the Irish traveled with tickets paid for by their British landlords.

During the height of the famine, the British government had passed laws requiring landlords to help pay for relief efforts. The laws made landlords responsible for their tenants. The more people on a landlord's farm, the more he paid, so it was usually cheaper for him to buy their steerage tickets and send them away.

The Irish packed themselves into creaky ships to cross the Atlantic Ocean. These overcrowded ships were later called "coffin ships" because they

British landlords forced Irish farmers out of their homes when they could not pay rent. Bands of starving, homeless Irish wandered the countryside, searching for food to eat, including diseased potatoes.

were barely able to sail and they often reached their destinations only after losing half the passengers to disease or hunger. Some ships were so full of people that they sank within a few days of leaving Ireland. There were no beds; passengers slept on their folded clothes. The food and water were usually unfit for consumption.

During the famine, Ireland lost a third of its population. Altogether, more than one million people died of either famine or disease—500,000 in 1847 alone. Nearly two million people came to the United States between 1845 and 1855, reducing Ireland's population from almost 9 million to just over 5 million. A letter written in 1850 from a young immigrant in New York City to her father in Ireland, described the life many Irish immigrants hoped to find in the United States. She wrote,

> *. . . any man or woman without a family are [sic] fools that would not venture and come to this plentiful Country where no man or woman ever hungered or ever will.*

The United States seemed to offer work, land, food, wages, freedom, and the right to participate in government—all things unavailable to the Irish in their homeland.

Thinking It Over

1. What made the potato such a dependable source of food?
2. **Drawing Conclusions** Why do you think the British continued to export meat and grain from Ireland while so many Irish starved?

2 City Life in the United States

Between 1820 and 1850, people from Ireland made up 42 percent of all immigrants to the United States. Most of the Irish were young, averaging between 15 and 35 years old, and more than half were women. Most arrived penniless, starving, poorly educated, and unskilled.

At the time the Irish arrived, only 15 percent of the U.S. population lived in cities. But that soon changed. Between 1845 and 1855, almost one million Irish, fleeing the potato famine, landed in New York City. Many of these Irish went to live in cities in Pennsylvania and Ohio. Other Irish immigrants arrived in Boston, Baltimore, and New Orleans. By 1870, 72 percent of Irish Americans lived in Massachusetts, Connecticut, New York, Pennsylvania, New Jersey, Ohio, and Illinois.

In the cities, the Irish stuck together and formed communities. They were attracted to city life because it offered something more dependable than the farming life they had left behind. There were many jobs available in industries for unskilled laborers. Irish men built canals, roads, sewers, bridges, railroads, and new housing. They helped the country to expand—and U.S. cities to flourish. Commenting on the large numbers of Irish entering the work force, one newspaper declared,

> *There are several sorts of power working at the fabric of this Republic—water power, steam power, and Irish power. The last works hardest of all.*

The Irish were the only immigrant group in which women, especially single women, outnumbered men. For these women, becoming a domestic servant was a popular career choice. More than 60 percent of working Irish immigrant women labored as servants. Irish servants could earn 50 percent more money than could saleswomen and 25 percent more than textile workers. Because they lived with the families for whom they worked, these women had no expenses for food, housing, or transportation. In addition, they did not have to live in the crowded apartments where most factory workers lived. Irish women saved their money and sent it to their families in Ireland. In fact, most of the money that families in Ireland received came from working Irish women and not from men.

Shantytowns

The drawback to city life, as Patrick and Bridget Kennedy had discovered, was its cost. Many Irish immigrants, with little money for housing, were forced to live in inexpensive areas close to where they worked. As a result, large groups of Irish settled in what became known as **shantytowns**, crowded, unsanitary areas where large immigrant families lived in basements and small, poorly constructed shacks.

Poverty and living conditions in shantytowns bred crime, alcoholism, and disease—especially cholera, which spread rapidly through the crowded homes. In New York, the mortality rate for Irish infants approached 80 percent. In Boston, 60 percent of the city's Irish children didn't live beyond the age of five.

In some places, the Irish organized to struggle against harsh living conditions. For example, in New York City, they formed the Convention of Irish Societies in 1851. This group collected dues and spoke to factory owners about improving the working conditions. The dues were used to help sick and disabled Irish immigrants.

Active Learning: As you read, take notes on the living conditions Irish immigrants endured and on the prejudice they experienced. You will want to use some of this information in your article.

A Cold Reception

Native-born Americans, most of whom were Protestants of British descent, reacted with suspicion toward the Irish, who were mostly Catholic. Because they were the first large-scale immigrant group to arrive in the United States, native-born Americans saw them as a threat to the "American" way of life.

Native-born Americans were intolerant and distrustful of Irish manners and lifestyles—which were very different from their own. One journalist portrayed the prejudice many felt, when he described the Irish as "jolly, reckless, good-natured, passionate, priest-ridden, whiskey-loving, thriftless . . . " In contrast, he found Yankees to be "cold, shrewd, frugal . . . "

Because they lived in such poor conditions, the Irish quickly became stereotyped as lazy, drunken, hot-tempered, and ignorant. Newspapers frequently ran jokes, stories, and cartoons that portrayed the negative aspects of life in Irish shantytowns. Native-born Americans also accused the Irish of being clannish because they preferred to live in Irish communities and to educate their children in Catholic schools.

As a result of these perceptions, anti-Irish and anti-Catholic prejudices flourished throughout the country and fueled violence in many cities, often causing riots. Catholic churches and convents were often burned. Many employers advertised their jobs with the words "No Irish Need Apply." Typical of the time was the following advertisement, which appeared in the *Daily Sun*, on May 11, 1853,

> *Woman wanted—To do general housework . . . English, Scotch, Welsh, German, or any country or color except Irish.*

Only after new ethnic groups began to arrive in the United States in the 1860s did the Irish begin

This cartoon shows how many people felt when large numbers of Irish came during the potato famine. Uncle Sam is the United States. He is telling Great Britain to send some of the Irish to Canada.

to rise in status. Their distinguished service in the Civil War, fighting heroically for both the North and the South, also helped speed their acceptance into U.S. society.

Fitting In

Among the first to appreciate the Irish immigrants were local politicians. They discovered that the Irish often voted as a group for a particular candidate. A candidate for political office would try very hard to convince the Irish community that he had their best interests at heart. Irish immigrants—English-speaking and white—had little trouble gaining citizenship and the right to vote. Their citizenship and voting rates were the highest of all immigrant groups.

Politicians who won Irish votes rewarded Irish communities by providing them with needed services and with jobs in fire departments, police departments, and other public service organizations, as well as with positions in utilities, subways, and railways that the city owned. By 1900, the Irish represented 30 percent of the municipal employees in New York City, Boston, and Chicago.

Many Irish also joined labor unions as a way to gain respect. They participated at both the local and national level, becoming leaders in such organizations as the Knights of Labor and the American Federation of Labor (AFL). In the 1890s, Irish labor leaders directed about half the labor unions in the AFL. As the Irish gained power in labor unions, they worked to bring about higher wages, shorter workdays, and safer working conditions for Irish Americans and other immigrant groups.

From positions as members of unions and public servants, it was a short step to more ambitious government roles. Unions often supported particular candidates and asked their members to vote for those politicians; in many elections, these candidates were Irish. In addition, with support from Irish communities willing to vote for one of their own, Irish politicians quickly assumed control of large Eastern cities such as New York City, Boston, and Chicago, thus establishing a foundation from which to build even greater political power.

Thinking It Over

1. Why did Irish immigrants tend to settle in cities?
2. **Making Inferences** Why do you think union membership helped the Irish take a greater part in politics?

3 Building Political Power

In large cities, groups of politicians came to be known as **machines**, informal but powerful organizations. These organizations combined dealmaking, arm-twisting, and community activism. Men who had become successful in business and who had been raised in Irish shantytowns were often the leaders of Irish political machines. These men were called **bosses**.

The political machines provided favors and services to Irish immigrant neighborhoods in exchange for their loyalty at the polls. Residents in need of a job, legal aid, help with medical expenses, even coal on a cold winter's night, would appeal to the bosses who would use their influence to help them. In return, the residents would give their votes and those of any friends they could persuade.

Irish political machines fought back against anti-Catholic prejudice by appointing Irish Americans to jobs in education and public service. They also gave public works projects to Irish building contractors, who, by 1870, accounted for 20 percent of all contractors in the country. The Irish contractors, in turn, hired Irish subcontractors and workers. Through these jobs, favors, and services, Irish politicians helped their communities overcome discrimination and improve their situation.

Irish politicians used political power as a tool to help their people rise out of poverty and into the middle class—and it worked. By 1900, 75 percent of the 1.2 million Irish men in blue-collar jobs were classified as skilled laborers. Irish women were

In 1911, the Triangle Shirtwaist Factory fire changed Smith's political career. In that fire, 146 female factory workers died. Smith joined the New York State Factory Commission, which was set up to investigate the fire. He was upset to discover that both women and children had been burned in the fire and that child labor was being used in the garment industry throughout the city. When Smith learned that working conditions for child laborers were worse than the conditions on the Lower East Side where he had grown up, he began to push for state laws that would make workplaces safer. Together with colleagues Robert Wagner, Sr., and Frances Perkins, who later became Secretary of Labor under the administration of President Franklin D. Roosevelt, he issued a landmark report that marked a turning point in government regulation of industry, housing, and child labor. The committee's report forced the state legislature to pass laws that improved working conditions.

In 1918, Smith became governor of New York and was reelected for four terms. While Smith was governor, he supported reforms that helped poor people. Under Smith's leadership, New York State passed laws that helped people pay their rent, provided hospital care for those who couldn't afford it, and set price limits on utilities such as electric and telephone service.

In 1928, Smith ran for President on the Democratic ticket. Nicknamed the "Happy Warrior," Smith was a popular candidate and many people believed he had a good chance of winning. However, anti-Catholic prejudice remained strong, and organizations such as the Ku Klux Klan spoke out against him. Smith lost the election; Americans were not yet ready to accept an Irish Catholic President.

Thinking It Over

1. How did the Irish political machines operate?
2. **Making Comparisons** How were the reform ideas of James Michael Curley and Al Smith similar?

4 The Ultimate Victory

By the 1930s, Irish Catholics were more successful than any other immigrant group at the time—politically and otherwise. They were visible in unions, sports, banking, entertainment, publishing, education, and many other industries. While they had not captured the presidency, Irish Catholics held powerful positions as campaign managers, speech writers, and advisers to presidents. For example, many Irish people worked for President Franklin D. Roosevelt. He chose Irish Americans as ambassadors, attorney generals, and cabinet members. His campaign manager, Irish American James Farley, even wrote notes in green ink.

Franklin D. Roosevelt chose Joseph Kennedy—grandson of famine immigrant Patrick Kennedy—as ambassador to Great Britain. Kennedy had become a bank president at the age of 25 and, through investments in the stock market, he became a millionaire 10 years later. Now he was the first Catholic and the first Irish man to serve as ambassador to Great Britain. He enjoyed this position immensely, especially for the discomfort it gave to London's anti-Irish establishment. Kennedy wanted a career in politics. However, just as the United States was about to enter World War II against Germany and Japan, Kennedy's political plans ended. During an interview, Kennedy took an unpopular stand when he recommended that the United States should avoid war by allowing Adolf Hitler, the German dictator, to take over Europe. Because his own political career was over, Kennedy wanted very much to see one of his sons become President.

Taking the White House

At first, Joseph Kennedy put his political energies behind his oldest son, Joseph, Jr. But when Joseph, Jr. was killed in combat during World War II, he turned his attention to John, the next in line. John Fitzgerald Kennedy, who was born on May 29, 1917, had also fought in World War II and was well-known for his heroic deeds. With his family's support, he made a swift and successful shift into politics.

In 1960, crowds often became excited when John F. Kennedy campaigned against Richard Nixon for President of the United States. Kennedy won by fewer than 115,000 votes.

In 1946, John began his political career by winning a seat in the U.S. House of Representatives, where he served for 6 years as a representative from Massachusetts. In 1952, he was elected to the U.S. Senate. Then, in 1960, he began his race for the highest political office in the United States—the presidency.

Many of the established Irish politicians doubted the country would vote for an Irish Catholic candidate. At first, they refused to support him. But John was youthful, aggressive, charming, intelligent, and witty. An eloquent speaker, he made passionate and persuasive speeches during which he lobbied for improved wages and working conditions, more public housing, and civil rights. He quickly became popular. For laborers, Irish Americans, Catholics, and other religious and ethnic groups, he represented a chance for equality.

John Kennedy's election as the thirty-fifth President of the United States—just over a century after his great-grandfather Patrick had died of cholera—was a triumph. He was the country's youngest elected President and its first Irish Catholic President. His victory raised the perception of what Irish Catholic Americans could achieve.

Today, many Irish Americans—Catholic and otherwise—continue to serve in key political positions. Many also serve as attorneys and judges, such as Supreme Court Justices William G. Brennan and Sandra Day O'Connor, the first woman appointed to the U.S. Supreme Court.

Overall, the Irish American contribution to politics was more positive than negative. Irish Americans had a view of life based on survival—they would work hard to get things done. Their conflict with Great Britain had also made them more aware of how important it is for the people of a country to make decisions on how their own country should be run.

Many Irish believed that taking part in politics was their right. Their experience in Ireland had taught them firsthand about the dangers of a system of government that did not allow everyone to take part. They preferred a more open government, one that welcomed people of different backgrounds. As far as they were concerned, an immigrant's son had as much leadership ability as a college-educated lawyer. Their organizations were eager to win support from all levels of society, from the wealthiest to the poorest. They brought citizens into the political process who had never before felt a part of it. As Tammany boss Richard Croker commented,

> *If we go down into the gutter, it is because there are men in the gutter, and you have got to go where they are if you are going to do anything with them.*

Thinking It Over

1. What did John F. Kennedy's presidency mean to the Irish American community?
2. **Making Inferences** What do you think were some of the characteristics of the Irish that made them struggle to succeed in politics?

GOING TO THE SOURCE

A Nation of Immigrants

President John F. Kennedy understood well the importance of immigration to the United States. His ancestors had come to the United States to escape the potato famine in Ireland. In his book *A Nation of Immigrants*, written before he became president, Kennedy wrote the passage that follows. Read the passage and then answer the questions below it.

> *The continuous immigration of the nineteenth and early twentieth centuries . . . gave every old [established] American a standard by which to judge how far he had come and every new American a realization of how far he might go. It reminded every American, old and new, that change is the essence of life, and that American society is a [ongoing] process, not a conclusion. . . . More than that, it infused [put into] the nation with a commitment to far horizons and new frontiers, and thereby kept the pioneer spirit of American life, the spirit of equality and of hope, always alive and strong.*

—From *A Nation of Immigrants* by John F. Kennedy.
New York: Harper & Row 1964 (original: 1958)

1. According to Kennedy, how does immigration benefit established Americans?
2. **Analyzing** What do you think Kennedy means when he says that "change is the essence of life?"
3. **Drawing Conclusions** In what ways do you think immigration affects the "spirit of hope" in the United States?

Case Study Review

Identifying Main Ideas

1. Why did so many Irish immigrants come to the United States in the mid 1800s?
2. How did native-born Americans react to this flood of Irish immigrants?
3. In what way did Irish immigrants influence local and national politics?

Working Together

Discuss the ways in which the United States government responds to national emergencies, such as helping victims of natural disasters. Then work together to make a list of emergency measures that the British government could have taken to assist Irish farmers during the Great Famine.

Active Learning

Write an Article Review the notes you took while reading this case study. Use your information to write a newspaper article about Irish American struggles and triumphs. Include information about why the Irish left their homeland, their early experiences in America, and their significant political achievements. Revise your draft as necessary, and give your article an appropriate headline.

Lessons for Today

When thousands of poor, uneducated Irish immigrants began to arrive in U.S. cities, native-born Americans reacted with suspicion and prejudice. Use library or media resources to find an example of a recent immigrant group that has faced prejudice and discrimination. How is your example similar to that of the Irish? How is it different?

What Might You Have Done?

Imagine that you live during the time when James Michael Curley was governor of Massachusetts—or when Al Smith was governor of New York. What might be some problems that existed in living or working conditions? How would you advise these leaders about the reforms that are needed in your state or community? Write a short paragraph about what you would say.

CRITICAL THINKING

Evaluating Conflicting Perspectives

Sometimes people view the same event differently. For example, when the Great Famine occurred, the views of British leaders were not the same as the views held by the Irish or even by those who went to Ireland to view the results of the famine. Read the following statements that were made during the Great Famine. Then, on another sheet of paper, answer the questions that follow.

> *"Russia wants liberty. Switzerland wants religion. Spain wants a king. Ireland alone wants food."*
>
> —*The Vindicator* [newspaper], 1846

> *"The problem of Ireland being altogether beyond the power of man, the cure has been applied by all-wise Providence [God]."*
>
> —Lord John Russell, Prime Minister of England, 1846

> *"For the poverty and distress and misery which exist, the people have themselves to blame."*
>
> —Thomas Campbell Foster, who investigated conditions in Ireland, 1846

> *"My hands tremble while I write. The scenes of human misery still haunt me. I entered a cabin. Stretched in one corner, scarcely visible, from the smoke and rags that covered them, were three children, lying there because they were too weak to rise—eyes sunk, voice gone, in the last stage of starvation. On some straw was a shriveled old woman, moving her arms to show how the skin hung loose from the bones. There was a young woman with sunken cheeks—a mother—who pressed her hand upon her forehead, with a look of anguish and despair. . . . "*
>
> —William Bennett, who observed the starvation in Ireland, 1847

> *"Even in London there is 'mortality' and the very best-fed men will die . . . and shall Ireland be exempt from the doom of man?"*
>
> —Queen Victoria, 1847

> *"I saw the family. They were skeletons, all of them, with skin on their bones and life within the skin. A mother skeleton and baby skeleton; a tall boy skeleton who had no work to do; who could do nothing but eat, and had nothing to eat. Four female children skeletons and the tall father skeleton, not able to work to get food and not able to get enough food when he did work."*
>
> —Alexander Somerville, 1847

1. **Analyzing** What does Lord John Russell say has caused the famine in Ireland?
2. **Analyzing** What is Queen Victoria's point of view? Explain her statement in your own words.
3. **Comparing and Contrasting** How does Queen Victoria's point of view contrast with the observations made by Bennett and Somerville?
4. **Drawing Conclusions** Why do you think many of the speakers expressed different points of view about the famine?

In garment factories, immigrants often worked where lint-filled air, piles of cloth, and oil-soaked machines created a fire hazard.

CASE STUDY 6

IMMIGRANTS INFLUENCE LABOR REFORM

CRITICAL QUESTIONS

- In what way did immigration contribute to labor abuses?
- When did public opinion about labor begin to change?

TERMS TO KNOW

- task force
- industrial revolution
- manufactured
- labor contractors
- sweatshops
- piecework
- unions
- reform
- scrip
- strike
- scabs

ACTIVE LEARNING

This case study focuses on the immigrant experience in factories, coal mines, and other U.S. industries, as well as the immigrants' struggle to improve working conditions in those jobs. Newspapers often ran political cartoons that expressed opinions about the labor movement. As you read this case study, write down what kind of cartoon you would draw about the labor movement. The Active Learning boxes will suggest ideas for you to illustrate.

It was 4:30 in the afternoon on March 25, 1911, and Irene Seivos was ending another long week of work at the Triangle Shirtwaist Company, a large clothing factory in New York City. As soon as Irene completed the day's work, she could leave the building for fresher air and enjoy what remained of her Saturday evening.

As Irene tried to focus on her sewing, she realized that something was wrong. A sharp smell of smoke filled the air. Something in the workroom was on fire. The fire spread rapidly through bolts of oil-soaked cloth; within minutes, the entire eighth floor burst into flames.

Everyone was in a panic, trying to escape from the fire. Irene ran to the stairway, but the door wouldn't open. The employers had locked it in order to keep out thieves and union workers. Next, Irene ran to the elevator. Later, she recalled,

> *Some of the girls were clawing at the elevator doors and crying, "Stop. Stop! For God's sake stop!" It was so hot we could barely breathe. When the elevator finally stopped and the door opened at last, my dress was on fire.*

Although others struggled to push her aside, Irene managed to jump into the crowded elevator. She said,

> *Someone grabbed my hair, which was long, and tried to pull me out. But I kicked free just as the doors closed.*

Irene was one of the lucky ones; she made it safely out of the burning building. Of 800 workers trapped inside, 146 died. Some tried to save themselves by jumping from the eighth and ninth floor windows, but almost all died instantly when they hit the sidewalk below. Some died when they became trapped in locked stairways and fire escapes. Still others burned to death while sitting at their machines.

Reports of the fire spread quickly. People were horrified. Almost 80,000 people marched

The Triangle Shirtwaist Company fire was one of the worst disasters in the history of New York City. Because the factory's owners had violated safety regulations, this tragic event brought about stricter laws to make workplaces safer.

A Good Book to Read

Lyddie by Katherine Paterson. New York: Puffin Books, 1991.

This engrossing novel tells the story of Lyddie Worthen, a poor farm girl who takes a job in a Massachusetts mill. Lyddie's experiences inside the loud, lint-filled mill offer a close-up look at this fast-paced, poorly paid, and dangerous work, as well as at the struggle that workers faced when trying to unionize.

silently in New York City in a mass funeral to mourn the victims. In response to the tragedy, the state of New York set up a **task force**, a group of experts organized to solve a specific problem, to study factory working conditions. Their report convinced the New York state legislature to pass laws that abolished labor by children under age 14, established strict time codes, including a 54-hour maximum workweek for women and children, and banned work on Sunday.

1 Cheap Labor

During the mid-1800s, the United States experienced an **industrial revolution**, a rapid change in how goods were produced. Products that had been made at home by hand were now **manufactured**, or produced with the help of machines and power tools, usually in factories that made them in large numbers.

As industries developed, millions of jobs became available. Business owners needed workers to operate the machines that made the fabric, clothing, clocks, sewing machines, and other items increasingly in demand. Between 1869 and 1914, the total number of workers employed in manufacturing tripled, increasing from two million to six million. Many of these workers were immigrants.

Often, immigrants came to this country with no skills and little or no money. Some discovered that the skills they brought were useless in the face of American technology. In both cases, they needed whatever jobs they could find. Industrial jobs required few, if any, specialized skills.

By 1910, immigrants accounted for over one half of America's industrial workers, although they made up only 14 percent of the population. Besides working in manufacturing, immigrants also labored in mining, railroad, and agricultural industries.

Most immigrants relied on family connections to help them find work. Because of this situation, certain industries became associated with particular ethnic groups: Scandinavians went into farming; Slavic groups worked in mines and steel mills; European Jews entered the garment industry. As Max Brossman, a Russian Jewish immigrant, recalled,

> *You came together with your own group. They found a place for you to live and a place for you to work.*

Long Hours, Low Pay

Unfortunately, most industrial jobs were difficult and low-paying. Like the Triangle Shirtwaist building, almost all factories were loud, dirty, and dangerous. In New York City, the largest number of people were employed in the textile industry, which accounted for 47 percent of the city's factories. Immigrants worked in stuffy, overcrowded rooms with poor lighting and fast-running machines that often caused injuries.

They worked 11- to 12- hour days, 6 days a week—and sometimes more. Pauline Newman, a young immigrant who worked in a clothing factory, recalls that,

> *In the busy season, we worked seven days a week. That's why the sign went up… "If You Don't Come In On Sunday, Don't Come In On Monday."*

On top of all this, workers earned only $1 to $2 a day. In contrast, middle class workers earned about $4.50 a day. Women usually performed the least skilled work and earned about half the wages that men earned.

Things weren't much better for immigrants in other industries. John Lukasavicius, a Lithuanian immigrant who worked in the Pennsylvania coal mines, recalls,

> *Working in the mine was hard and dangerous. Every day someone was getting hurt. During the three weeks I spent there, I never saw the sunlight, because we went down in the mine before the sun came out and we finished work after the sun had set.*

Coal miners in Pennsylvania and West Virginia worked 10 hours a day, 6 and a half days a week in highly dangerous surroundings, risking cave-ins, explosions, and other hazards. For their work, they earned from 60 cents to $2.50 per day.

In California and Oregon, immigrants who labored in the canning industry also worked long hours for low pay in hazardous conditions. They stood all day in damp, dirty sheds, from 3 A.M. until late afternoon, using razor-sharp knives to shuck oysters and peel shrimp. The odor from the seafood stung their noses and eyes, the lighting was dim, and the liquid in the shrimp was so strong that it caused their fingers to swell and ate holes in their shoes. They worked so quickly that workers frequently cut their fingers with their knives.

Speaking after the Shirtwaist Company tragedy, Rose Schneiderman, a Russian-Polish immigrant who worked in factories from age 13, commented on how workers were treated. She said,

> *The life of men and women is so cheap and property is so sacred. There are so many of us for one job, it matters little if 140-odd are burned to death.*

Looking to make the largest profit possible, employers refused to spend money to improve working conditions. During hard times, many industries further slashed workers' already low pay rather than take a loss themselves.

Sweatshops

With such low wages, immigrants could work all day every day and still not earn enough to support their families. In order to make money to buy food or pay rent, entire families had to work. In the textile industry, many people worked in their homes, where parents, children, and other relatives labored side by side, seven days a week, sewing clothes, stitching collars, making feather goods, and doing other repetitive tasks. Recalls Sando Bologna, the son of Italian immigrants,

> *All the kids sat around the table. They didn't go out to play unless they did their quota. . . . and sometimes they didn't eat until they finished.*

Children who didn't perform these tasks would cook, clean, and care for their younger brothers and sisters. Families also earned money by taking in laundry or by opening their homes to boarders. Sometimes women worked outside the home, taking jobs as maids, field hands, or factory workers. However, women workers were paid even less than men—about one-half to two-thirds as much—for the same work.

Some immigrants became **labor contractors**, people who hired extra workers in order to take on large assignments. They turned their apartments into small cramped factories called **sweatshops**, where men, women, and children worked from morning until night as quickly as they could. Labor contractors would go directly to immigration stations, looking for newly-arrived immigrants whom they would hire as cheap labor. In 1914, about 60 percent of all businesses were small shops, employing fewer than 30 workers.

This woman and her daughters worked in their home doing piecework. Their job was to sew pants for a clothing manufacturer. They might make about 40 cents for a dozen pair of pants.

Competition among contractors was fierce. In order to win jobs, they bid low prices. Much of their work came from clothing manufacturers who cut costs by dividing sewing tasks into small sections, or **piecework**, such as sleeves, belts, hems, and buttonholes. They hired out this piecework to sweatshops and families. Labor contractors, whose profit depended on the number of pieces they produced, pushed immigrants to work faster and faster, yet paid them only pennies a day.

Jacob Riis, a Danish immigrant who was a photographer and social reformer, wrote in his book *How the Other Half Lives,*

> *The bulk of the sweater's [labor contractor's] work is done in the tenements, which the law that regulates factory labor does not reach. The child works unchallenged from the day he is old enough to pull a thread. There is no such thing as a dinner hour. Men and women eat while they work, and the "day" is lengthened at both ends far into the night.*

Active Learning: Your political cartoon might comment on the sweatshop situation. You could focus on the length of the workday or on the labor contractors who met unsuspecting immigrants just hours after they arrived in the country.

Child Labor

Many workers were just children. Although some states had laws against hiring children younger than 14, these laws were largely ignored. Employers hired children because they were cheap and easy to control; and parents, desperate to make a living, often lied about a child's age. Recalls Pauline Newman, who started working in the garment industry when she was eight years old,

> *Somehow the employer knew when the inspector was coming. Materials came in high wooden cases, and when the inspector came, we were put into them and covered with shirtwaists. By the time he arrived, there were no children.*

Children worked in sweatshops, factories, seafood canneries, crop fields, and coal mines. They made deliveries, sold newspapers, stacked firewood, and shined shoes. Records show that by 1910, more than two million children between the ages of 10 and 15 were employed—making up close to 20 percent of the labor force. Many younger children were employed as well.

The jobs children did were repetitive and dangerous. The accident rate for working children was three times that of adults. They suffered severed fingers, broken bones, deep gashes, and heat exhaustion. They fell into coal chutes and died. For all their hard work, most earned only pennies a day and had little time or energy left for school. They were forced to sacrifice their health, their education, and their future for next to nothing.

Even children who didn't work full time found jobs before or after school. In thinking about his first job at the age of 12, making morning deliveries for a bakery, Leonard Covello, an Italian immigrant, recalls,

In the 1880s, young children often worked in factories. Working in a cotton mill, these boys changed spindles in a textile machine.

At four-thirty every morning, I walked rapidly over to the bakery shop. There the day's orders were waiting for me to be put into bags for delivery. . . . It was rush, rush, rush, back and forth from the bakery until all the orders were delivered. Then I had to run home and get ready for school. For this work I received one dollar and seventy-five cents a week.

Thinking It Over

1. What type of work was available to immigrants with few skills?
2. **Analyzing** What negative effects did child labor have on childhood and on society in general?

2 Struggles and Protest

As the low pay, dangerous conditions, and poor treatment continued, immigrants and other workers throughout the country became increasingly frustrated. They realized there was little they could accomplish individually. Searching for ways to improve their lot, they began joining **unions**, groups of workers who are joined together to protect and improve their work arrangements.

Unions offered workers a chance to talk about their frustrations and to discuss plans for bringing about **reform**, or improvements, in the workplace. They also offered opportunities to socialize and gave workers a feeling of hope for the future.

Some unions offered benefits to workers who went on strike, such as food and shelter for evicted workers and their families. As unions grew in size and strength, many established other benefits as well—food-buying cooperatives, insurance, resource libraries, and lectures. Most importantly, unions meant bargaining power. Unions could pressure employers to make improvements, such as higher wages, shorter workdays, and safer working conditions.

Joining the Unions

Unions have existed since the mid-1800s, but they took a while to develop. The employer knew that if workers joined unions, they could make demands that would cost money. Employers did their best to squash the unions and threatened to fire workers who joined.

Some companies tried to persuade workers to join company-run unions, as a Scottish immigrant recalls,

When the company saw how fast the workers were signing union cards, they started to organize a company union. . . . [T]he president of the company . . . [would] tell us that if we'd stick by him, we'd get a 10 percent bonus and everything else. Then he wouldn't sign even a company agreement . . . He wanted us to take his word by mouth. Instead of gaining with the workers, he lost out . . . We demanded a . . . wage increase . . . We won vacations with pay, seniority rights, recognition of the union as . . . bargaining agent, time and a half for overtime, sanitation improvements. We gained a lot.

Once workers learned just how powerful independent unions could be, enrollment quickly increased. At first, many unions refused to welcome immigrants. Union members saw them as a threat to American workers and as the main cause of low wages. One union that accepted all workers—immigrant or native born, skilled or unskilled—was the Knights of Labor. But few other unions would represent unskilled laborers. However, immigrants represented a major segment of the labor force, and unions soon realized that they needed them in order to survive. They realized that they could accept immigrants to increase their power and at the same time fight for immigration control.

A number of immigrants went on to become respected leaders in the labor reform movement, such as Samuel Gompers, a British immigrant who cofounded the American Federation of Labor (AFL). As a child, Gompers had worked for pennies a day rolling cigars to help support his family. He began his union career by organizing a local cigar makers' union and soon worked to establish larger, more powerful unions, such as the

AFL, an organization composed of skilled workers in craft unions.

Union organizers brought together men and women of many nationalities and convinced them to work together. John Mitchell, president of the United Mine Workers, told his members that,

> *The coal you dig isn't Slavish, or Polish, or Irish coal, it's just coal.*

Still, despite their growing numbers, unions faced tremendous opposition. Business owners were powerful people with powerful connections. During disputes, most city and state officials lined up on the side of business. At times, business owners took extreme measures to protect their interests.

Active Learning: You might sketch out ideas for a political cartoon that comments on the growth of unions. You could focus on the resistance by unions to accept immigrants or on the resistance by employers to accept unions.

The Ludlow Massacre

In the coal fields of southern Colorado, immigrant miners from Greece, Italy, and Mexico worked long dangerous days. For 12 hours, 6 to 7 days a week, they toiled in deep underground tunnels, risking death and injury from explosions and cave-ins. Their pay depended on how much coal they dug out of the mines. Often, the miners were cheated by the company men who weighed their coal.

The Colorado Fuel and Iron Company, for which they worked, owned their homes and all the land, schools, churches, and stores in the area. The miners and their families were forced to live in run down, unsanitary homes and to pay outrageous prices for food and supplies. If they shopped at any other stores, they were fired.

Workers, who earned only 63 cents a day, were paid in **scrip**, certificates good toward supplies at company-owned stores. Each week, company owners deducted food, rent, and utilities from their wages, leaving little or nothing on which to live. This arrangement kept mining families in poverty and debt, unable to get ahead no matter how hard they tried. When miners were injured or killed on the job, families were not compensated, and if they were unable to pay their rent, they were evicted.

In September 1913, more than 10,000 Colorado miners went on **strike**, refusing to work until employers met their demands for higher wages, better conditions, and the right to join the union. The Colorado Fuel and Iron Company responded by evicting strikers from their homes and hiring **scabs**, or replacement workers, to fill their jobs. When strikers marched to demand changes in the mines, they were beaten by thugs

GOOD FOR

FIVE CENTS.

IN MERCHANDISE AT

STORE 20.

GOOD ONLY TO AN EMPLOYE ON ACCOUNT OF LABOR PERFORMED

THE COLUMBUS & HOCKING COAL & IRON CO.

Per

Colorado miners weren't paid with money. They were paid in scrip, pieces of paper that they could use to exchange for supplies at the company-owned store. This scrip is worth five cents.

hired by the coal company and arrested by police. Even the state militia was called in.

But strikers refused to back down. They moved their families into the mountains, where the United Mine Workers Union had set up tents. Some of these tent communities were in the company-owned town of Ludlow.

Tensions between the owners and the strikers increased. Finally, in April 1914, the militia turned vicious. The soldiers tossed bombs into the Ludlow tent community and then shot at people as they attempted to flee. Later, they set fire to the strikers' tents. By the end of the day, 12 children, 2 women, and 5 men were dead.

Even the Ludlow Massacre, while enraging the public, did little to help workers at the time. By the following December, the coal company still had not backed down, and the union voted to end the strike. The miners returned to work, defeated—and with a cut in pay.

Setbacks

Unions faced many—often violent—conflicts before becoming an established part of the labor system. Many people feared socialist revolution, chaos, and disorder because of strikes, which often spun out of control. As more and more immigrants from communist and socialist countries joined unions, the fears of native-born Americans increased.

In general, socialists believed that when the economy was based on private ownership and free competition, the rich got richer and the poor got poorer. They felt that wealth should be evenly distributed among workers and that society as a whole should make labor decisions.

Although some unions did have socialist agendas, most were concerned only with improving wages and working conditions. However, employers used every opportunity to exploit public fears by playing up the connection between unionism and anti-government activity. Siding with employers, local courts issued orders to stop strikes and at times held strikers responsible for employers' financial losses during a strike. In general, courts usually viewed unions as part of a conspiracy to restrain trade.

The press sided with employers as well, frequently publishing anti-labor editorials and cartoons. As anti-labor hysteria increased, even unions that had been growing steadily over the years began to lose members—especially membership of native-born Americans, which dropped as unions became increasingly open to immigrants and minorities. Union membership declined from a peak of 4 million in 1918 to 2 million by the late 1920s.

After organizing miners in many other states, the United Mine Workers urged workers in Colorado to join the union. In 1914, a strike called by the union ended in death and destruction for many Ludlow miners.

Thinking It Over

1. How did coal companies benefit by controlling miners' living arrangements?
2. **Drawing Conclusions** Why were coal companies determined to defeat the unions?

3 Bringing About Change

Despite occasional defeats, unions saw strikes as one of their strongest weapons. Strikes brought the production of goods to a standstill and forced employers to admit that they depended on labor as much as labor depended on them.

Garment workers were among the most successful at using the strike. The year before the Triangle Shirtwaist Fire, 20,000 New York garment workers had gone on strike to demand better health and safety conditions, a 52-hour work week, and overtime pay.

Clara Lemlich, an outspoken Jewish immigrant worker who had been beaten on the picket line, urged her fellow strikers to continue the fight and led them in a pledge that solidified the protest:

> *If I turn traitor to the cause I now pledge, may this hand whither from the arm I now raise.*

Although the strike was settled without attention to worker safety, more than two-thirds of the industry's companies were forced to make some kind of settlement, and future strikes brought about even greater reforms. Victories such as these boosted union participation and further increased its power. An Italian immigrant recalled,

> *After the union came into Stamford Waist, I got an increase all right. . . . and no work on Saturdays. Besides that we only had to work until 4:00. Our hours were reduced from 44 to 35 hours a week. And we had better conditions. . . . We had the union behind us, and we were respected better than we were before we had it.*

Publicity surrounding a strike could also be effective. While the Ludlow Massacre failed to bring immediate relief to the strikers, it helped sway public opinion in their favor. Like the Triangle Fire three years earlier, it was a tragedy that shocked and horrified the nation.

News coverage of these and other events made people aware of the dangerous conditions and unfair treatment that laborers experienced. The public became more sympathetic to labor than it had been before, and reformers worked harder than ever to bring about change. Their efforts brought about new laws regarding work hours, unions, and health and safety in the workplace. Even conditions in the Colorado mines improved over the next few years.

Mother Jones and the March of the Mill Children

One of the most famous union organizers of all time was Mary Harris "Mother" Jones. An Irish immigrant, daughter of a railroad worker, and widow of an ironworker, Mother Jones knew firsthand how big business abused its workers. A feisty old woman with a sharp tongue, she became involved in the labor movement in the late 1800s. For more than 50 years, she traveled across the country helping workers to organize unions and to fight for their rights, often landing in jail for her efforts.

At the turn of the century Mother Jones turned her attention to child labor. "I wanted to see for myself if the [gruesome] stories of little children working in the mills were true," she wrote in her autobiography. She described the children as,

> *Little girls and boys, barefooted, walked up and down between endless rows of spindles. They reached their little hands into the machinery to repair snapped threads. They crawled under the machinery to oil it. Tiny babies of six years old with faces of sixty did an 8-hour shift for ten cents a day.*

Mother Jones was a master at publicity. She first drew attention to the horrors of child labor in 1903 by putting maimed children on display at City Hall in Philadelphia. These were children whose hands had been crushed by dangerous machinery or whose fingers snapped off. To the crowd that gathered she declared,

> *I charge that Philadelphia's mansions were built on the broken bones, the quivering hearts, and drooping heads of these little children.*

Newspapers reported on the event, but the publicity soon died down. In order to energize her campaign against child labor, Mother Jones organized a 125-mile March of the Mill Children from Philadelphia to President Theodore Roosevelt's home in New York. Along the way, she gave rousing speeches against child labor. Unfortunately, when the marchers reached their destination, the President refused to see them, saying he could not help.

While the march failed to accomplish all that Mother Jones had hoped, it did generate a great amount of publicity, informing the public about the terrible injustice of child labor. More and more educators, politicians, religious leaders, reporters, and other reformers began to speak out against it. The following year, the National Child Labor Committee (NCLC) was organized in New York City with the goal of investigating child labor abuses and fighting for new laws.

Mother Jones was a dynamic force as a labor leader. She continued to fight for the rights of workers even into her nineties.

Active Learning: Your political cartoon might focus on the protest against child labor practices. Your sketches could include wealthy employers and the young children they employed.

The Power of Pictures

In 1908, the NCLC hired Lewis Hine, a photographer and reformer, to help them in their cause. A Danish immigrant orphaned at 15, Hine himself had labored long and hard as a child. He could relate to the children he would photograph.

Over the course of 20 years, Hine took about 5,000 photographs of children working in mills, mines, factories, and fields. The NCLC used Hine's photos in its pamphlets and published them in magazines and newspapers. These pictures revealed the harsh realities of child labor—and, for many people, seeing was believing.

Still, reform came slowly. Pennsylvania, for example, required that working children be at least 13 years old and set their workweek at a maximum of 6 days a week, 10 hours per day. However, many parents lied about their children's ages, and Pennsylvania mills regularly employed children much younger than 13. By 1914, 35 states had similar laws, but as in Pennsylvania, they were largely ignored.

The NCLC and other reformers refused to give up. In 1916, their efforts led Congress to pass the Keating-Owen Act, which established national standards for child labor. The law set the minimum age for working children at 14, limited the workday to 8 hours, prohibited night work for children under 16, and required documented proof of age for employment. The act outlawed the transportation of goods produced by child labor across state lines. However, in 1918, the Supreme

In the late 1880s, children made up 20 percent of the labor force. They worked long hours in dangerous and unhealthy conditions. In 1890, these children worked in textile mills. Here, they have gone on strike for better and safer work conditions.

Court declared the law unconstitutional because it interfered with interstate commerce.

Bowing to continuing pressure from reformers, many states banned child labor and established maximum work hours. Between 1910 and 1920, the number of child laborers decreased by half. Finally, in 1938, Congress officially passed the Fair Labor and Standards Act, setting federal limits on child labor. In 1949, Congress passed an amendment to the law directly prohibiting child labor.

Although the Supreme Court was generally opposed to setting standards for child labor, the courts sometimes ruled in favor of other workers. In 1908, in the case of *Muller v. Oregon*, the Supreme Court ruled that a state could legally limit the working hours of women. In 1917, in the case of *Bunting v. Oregon*, the Supreme Court ruled in favor of a 10-hour workday for men.

The struggle to hold industry accountable—for all its workers—was long and hard. But as the immigrant population grew, unionized, and gained voting power, so too did its ability to bring about change. Unions such as the Mexican and Japanese Farm Workers Union, the United Mine Workers Union, the Union of Chinese and Japanese Miners, and countless others sprang up to represent just about every type of skilled and unskilled worker in the United States. The hard work and strength that immigrants provided to the labor movement led to workplace changes that benefited all Americans.

A National Labor Policy

Immigrants not only joined unions, they worked to organize them as well. Immigrant men such as Samuel Gompers were in the forefront of the labor reform movement. In addition, many immigrant women were involved. For example, Rose Schneiderman, a native of Russian Poland who worked in factories from age 13, established the first local chapter of the Jewish Socialist United Cloth, Hat, and Cap Makers Union, and she later became president of the New York Women's Trade Union League. Irish American Leonora O'Reilly joined the Knights of Labor at age 16, organized a female chapter of the United Garment Workers of America, and later joined the Women's Trade Union League. These and hundreds of other small and large unions gave strength to the labor movement.

Thinking It Over

1. Why did Mother Jones march from Philadelphia to New York?
2. **Drawing Conclusions** Why do you think it took pictures of children working in terrible conditions to spur change in child labor laws?

GOING TO THE SOURCE

Working in the Sweatshops

Immigrants' thoughts and feelings about their early lives in America have been collected in numerous books and oral histories. Many immigrants describe work experiences in stuffy, cramped tenement apartments, where they sewed garments or assembled various goods. These rooms were often referred to as "sweatshops" because of the long days and difficult work that went on there. The following poem, by Yiddish poet Morris Rosenfeld, vividly describes the sweatshop experience.

I work, and I work, without rhyme, without reason—
produce and produce, and produce without end.
For what? and for whom? I don't know, I don't wonder
—since when can a whirling machine comprehend?

No feelings, no thoughts, not the least understanding;
this bitter, this murderous drudgery drains
the noblest, the finest, the best and the richest,
the deepest, the highest that living contains.

Away rush the seconds, the minutes and hours;
each day and each night like a wind-driven sail;
I drive the machine, as though eager to catch them,
I drive without reason—no hope, no avail.

1. What descriptive words and phrases does the poet use to help you see and feel what working in a sweatshop was like?
2. **Analyzing** Do you think that sweatshops caused some immigrants to lose hope in the American Dream, the idea of working hard and achieving success? Why or why not?

Case Study Review

Identifying Main Ideas

1. What types of work were available to unskilled immigrants?
2. Why did many employers prefer to hire children?
3. How did unions help immigrants fight for their rights?

Working Together

Work with a partner to look in newspapers for five or six help wanted ads offering jobs appropriate for unskilled workers. Find out about the wages, benefits, and hours required for each job. Make a chart comparing the types of work available to unskilled workers today with the work available to them in the early 20th century.

Active Learning

Create a Political Cartoon A political cartoon makes a strong comment about a situation. Look at the ideas for sketches you wrote as you read this case study. Choose your strongest idea and then form a small group with two or three other students to share and discuss it. Suggest ways to make each person's idea stronger. Prepare a final sketch using the group's suggestions. Once all final sketches are ready, vote as a group to select one idea to develop into a finished cartoon. Work together to illustrate it.

Lessons for Today

The labor abuses that immigrant children faced are a part of American history. But you might be surprised to learn that similar abuses continue today. Thousands of children aged three and up work in America's crop fields and in garment industry sweatshops. Many are immigrants, and they are frequently underpaid. Why do you think these abuses continue to happen despite child labor laws? How do you think this situation affects the children? the country? Do you think it is possible to completely eliminate child labor?

What Might You Have Done?

Imagine that you are a newly arrived immigrant working hard to help your parents support your family. Co-workers approach you about joining their union to fight for better working conditions. You could be fired if your employer finds out about your involvement in the union. What would you do?

CRITICAL THINKING

Developing Fair-Minded Opinions

Having Intellectual Courage

Intellectual courage is the ability to keep an open mind and develop your own opinion about a situation. In doing so, it is important to consider what beliefs you hold. You may have ideas that are false or misleading. It takes courage to question your own attitudes and beliefs.

In order to develop a fair-minded opinion, you need to consider other points of view. Doing so helps you decide what you believe to be the truth.

Read the information about Mother Jones. Then answer the questions below.

Laborers loved Mary Harris Jones. They called her "Mother" Jones because of the work she did to help workers fight for their rights. Coal miners called her the "miners' angel."

Employers and government officials, on the other hand, despised Mother Jones. They called her a "busybody" and claimed that she stirred up their workers. Over and over, they threatened her, arrested her, and threw her in jail.

But Mother Jones never gave up. She held union meetings despite laws saying she couldn't. She used her age and the fact that she was a woman to help her in her cause, drumming up publicity almost everywhere she went.

One time, when asked where she lived, she replied:

I live wherever there is a good fight against wrong—all over the country.

Mother Jones was 100 years old when she died on November 30, 1930. But even into her nineties, Mother Jones kept her fighting spirit.

1. **Analyzing** Why do you think government officials supported the opinions of business owners?
2. **Synthesizing Information** What qualities helped Mother Jones in her fight to help laborers?
3. **Forming an Opinion** If most of your friends have a strong opinion about something, why is it difficult to disagree with them?

Discussion

In the past, many factory owners often refused to improve health and safety conditions in the workplace. Today, most business owners think that health and safety is a major concern. Why do people see things differently today? Will people look back at work conditions today and wonder how we could have accepted them? Why or why not?

The Cuban American National Council holds classes that help students learn to perform science experiments.

CASE STUDY 7

BUILDING COMMUNITIES

CRITICAL QUESTIONS

- How do community organizations such as the Cuban American National Council help immigrants adjust to life in a new country?
- How did the three waves of Cuban immigrants over the past 40 years create a need for a community organization?

TERMS TO KNOW

- dictator
- political refugees
- visas
- *balseros*

ACTIVE LEARNING

In this case study, you will learn about the ways in which a group of immigrants joined together to help the less fortunate in their community. You will compare the stories and the needs of certain groups in your community with those you read about, and develop a plan for helping groups in your community.

Federico Sealy's parents were worried. In school, Federico was barely passing. He was hanging around with the wrong crowd in the poor area of Miami where the family lived. Mr. Sealy, a house painter from the Dominican Republic, and Mrs. Sealy, a secretary, felt that if they did not take steps soon, their son would drop out of school.

As it happened, the Sealys reached a crisis point with their son at the same time as school administrators. Federico's failing grades had already forced them to remove Federico from the basketball team. Now his increasing absences forced school officials to make a decision—Federico had to find a different school. He would not graduate unless he did.

In the past, teenagers like Federico would have had few options. But fortunately for the Sealy family, the Cuban American National Council (CNC) was ready to help. The CNC is an organization that helps people in the Cuban community. Part of its mission is to operate the Little Havana Institute, four schools for Hispanic students in grades 7 through 12. Classes are small so students can receive more attention from instructors. Goals for each student are clearly set and counselors are ready to help when they are needed.

For Federico Sealy, the Little Havana Institute meant the difference between success and failure. Federico became a serious student and star athlete. He also enrolled in a community college after graduating and plans to become a physical education teacher.

For the CNC, Federico's success was another story with a happy ending. To understand the importance of community services, it is important to think about the Cuban community itself and the changes it has undergone.

In 1960, Hispanic people made up less than 5 percent of the population of the greater Miami area. Today, Miami is more than half Hispanic; in fact, Miami has the highest percentage of foreign-born residents of any city in the United States. As the number of immigrants has grown, the need for services has also expanded; and by taking on that role for the past 25 years, the CNC has made a dramatic difference in the lives of thousands of people like Federico Sealy.

1 The First Group of Cuban Immigrants

Although the CNC has been in existence for more than 25 years, the actual story of its origins begins much earlier. Late in 1958, Fulgencio Batista, the once-powerful **dictator**, or ruler, of Cuba fled the country. Batista had been in power since 1952, and his rule had meant strict military control of the Cuban people.

Batista's regime had led to a revolt under the leadership of Fidel Castro. In early January 1959, Castro and his rebel forces paraded past thousands of cheering Cubans in the streets of Havana. However, the joy at Castro's victory was short-lived. Within months after taking power, Castro had announced that Cuba would become a Communist country. The government would control all private businesses—factories, ranches, farms, restaurants, and stores. Clothing, food, and other staples of life would be distributed evenly among all the people.

Dreams of freedom from Batista faded quickly into the nightmare of a Communist country. Police demanded that all citizens show ID cards. No criticism of the government was allowed in newspapers, books, or on TV. The government also outlawed gatherings of people opposed to communism.

The "Golden Exiles"

As the 1960s dawned, Cuba drew the world's attention. The almost overnight transition of Castro from rebel hero to Communist dictator sent shock waves to many corners of the world, including the United States. In those days, the cold war between democratic governments and Communist countries was at its height. For a Communist government to be established in Cuba only 90 miles from U.S. shores made the cold war even worse. As a result, the United States wanted to weaken Castro's government if possible.

One way to weaken the government was to encourage Cubans to leave the country. Thus, instead of categorizing Cubans entering the United States as "immigrants" and limiting the number who could enter the country, the United States labeled Cubans who left their homeland as "**political refugees**"—people who had fled from a country for political reasons.

The first wave of Cuban refugees were those who had lost the most in the change to communism. Under Communist rule, people were not allowed to own property. The Castro government took over plantations, factories, and estates.

Among this group of Cuban immigrants were many professionals—business people, doctors, lawyers, ranchers, sugarcane growers, and others—whose property had been confiscated, or taken, by the Castro government. Despite their treatment at the hands of the Communists, these Cubans were known as the "golden exiles" because of their former status in Cuba. So many people left Cuba that in 1962, Castro stopped air flights between Cuba and the United States.

Freedom Flights

From 1962 until 1965, Cubans continued to leave their homeland in large numbers. However, as growing numbers of Cubans rejected communism, Castro began to tighten the restrictions that prevented people from emigrating from Cuba. **Visas**, or travel permits that allowed people to leave, and plane tickets for flights to countries such as Mexico or Spain—and then on to the United States—became difficult to obtain.

In 1965, Castro announced that Cubans who had relatives in the United States could leave Cuba by boat. Many Cubans in Florida hired boats to go to Cuba and to return with their relatives. However, many of the boats were not seaworthy, and this policy resulted in many deaths at sea.

To stop the loss of life, the governments of the United States and Cuba agreed to reestablish air flights between the two countries. During the next 8 years, the so-called Freedom Flights brought more than 300,000 Cubans to the United States to be reunited with loved ones.

Because Cubans had entered the United States as refugees rather than as immigrants, their numbers were not restricted. However, it was not clear how long the refugees would be able to remain in the United States.

In 1966, Congress passed the Cuban American Adjustment Act, which gave any Cuban who had lived in the United States for 1 year the right to become a permanent resident. This act has allowed hundreds of thousands of Cubans who arrived both before and after 1966 to become permanent residents, a privilege that has not been granted to any other immigrant group.

Active Learning: Make a list of the types of needs the "golden exiles" might have. Divide the list into three sections—immediate, such as clothing; intermediate, such as housing; and long term, such as employment. Fill in as many needs under each heading as you can.

Thinking It Over

1. Why were most Cubans joyful at Castro's victory?
2. **Making Inferences** Why might the Castro government have been glad to see many educated and professional people leave Cuba?

2 The Expanding Community

Between 1960 and 1970, the population of Cubans in Dade County, Florida—Miami and the surrounding areas—grew from 29,500 to 224,000 people. The people who had fled Cuba in the early 1960s were among the best-educated and wealthiest group of immigrants ever to enter the United States.

Some refugees—especially those who spoke English—were able to put their skills to work in banking, law, medicine, or other professional fields.

Many stores in Miami's Little Havana display signs in both English and Spanish. Spanish-speaking people make up more than half of Miami's population.

Most, however, were forced to take jobs below their abilities. Many people who had held powerful positions in Cuba were forced to take jobs as garment workers, gardeners, maids, and janitors. Those who did not speak English were at a special disadvantage when it came to finding work.

Despite the difficulties they encountered, Cuban refugees succeeded. Because many were well educated, they were able to rise quickly in their jobs once they learned English.

Little Havana

In the early 1960s, Eighth Street was part of a shabby, low-rent area of Miami. As planeload after planeload of Cuban refugees landed in Miami, the need for inexpensive housing grew critical. Refugee service agencies often placed families in the vicinity of Eighth Street because of the large numbers of low-cost apartments and houses available.

Soon, "Calle Ocho," the Spanish term for Eighth Street, was the heart of the refugee community. By the early 1970s, Cuban-owned businesses and stores began to spring up in the neighborhood, and the area surrounding "Calle Ocho" became known as Little Havana.

The rapid success of Cuban refugees was at first welcomed by many Americans in the Miami area. In 1973, Dade County passed a bilingual policy that required the use of both Spanish and English on all traffic signs and office buildings, as well as in public schools.

However as the wave of refugees continued to arrive, that welcome weakened. Many longtime Miami residents began to express resentment at those who did not speak English. By 1974, a school board candidate won a seat on the Miami Board of Education by pledging to halt bilingual education, even though more than 30 percent of all students spoke Spanish as their first language.

In 1973, a change in Cuba's emigration policy led to further complications in the refugee picture. That year, the Castro government again discontinued all direct flights between Cuba and the United States. But closing the airways only sent Cubans to the water to escape from communism.

Saving and Serving

Those who escaped from Cuba by sea were called ***balseros*** (rafters). The Straits of Florida in the Caribbean Sea became the main thoroughfare between Cuba and the United States. It was a dangerous route and for Cubans on flimsy craft with only the barest knowledge of sea travel, it was a deathtrap.

In addition to the dangers from Cuban shore patrols, *balseros* faced the cold, wounds, dehydration, starvation, and shark attacks. Some experts estimate that as many as 75 percent of those who attempted to escape from Cuba by sea died. This wave of *balseros* brought into the Cuban American community a new element of refugees. They were young, not well educated, and poor.

By the early 1970s, several forces for change were at work in the Cuban American community. Many Cuban Americans in the first wave of refugees were now established in the United States; many were American citizens. A large number thought of themselves as Cuban Americans rather than as simply Cubans.

The needs of the well-established Cuban American community were much different from those of the *balseros*. The *balseros* needed housing, job training, and education. The exiles who had been in the United States for several years often needed financial support, community leaders, and political representation at higher levels of government. Among both groups, however, were those whose adjustment problems were the most difficult—senior citizens and teenagers.

It was because of those needs that a group of Cuban Americans in 1972 established the Cuban American National Council (CNC) to save and to serve the community. Because the community had so many needs, the original aim of the CNC was to make recommendations for organizations to help Cuban Americans.

Active Learning: Try to imagine the steps that had to be taken in the Cuban American community to form Little Havana in the 1970s. Then describe the steps you would take to address the following questions: "What are the day-to-day problems you might face in helping Cuban exiles? How would you go about determining which needs are the greatest?"

Thinking It Over

1. How were the *balseros* that arrived in the United States in the mid-1970s different from the "golden exiles"?
2. **Making Inferences** Why might senior citizens and teenagers face the most serious adjustment problems among the refugees?

3 From Mariel to Miami

By the end of the 1970s, the established generation of Cuban American exiles had made Miami one of the most important cities in the Latin American world. With Spanish-language newspapers, TV networks, banks, and other businesses, Miami began to draw non-Cuban Hispanic immigrants from countries in the Caribbean and Latin America. In fact, with Hispanics making up about half of its population, Miami became known as the "capital city of the Caribbean."

At this time the CNC began to focus on job training, low-income housing, and the economic development of some areas in Dade County. Because of the various situations that forced Hispanic immigrants from their homelands, the CNC did not favor one political point of view over any other. Its primary mission was improvement in the quality of life for Cuban Americans and other Hispanic immigrants.

The Mariel Boatlifts

As the 1970s ended, the CNC was beginning to build a name as an effective organization working for change. Then, in 1980, the Castro government again caused turmoil in Cuba and the United States. That year, Castro opened up the port of Mariel to boats from the United States. Anyone who wished to journey from the United States to Cuba could transport relatives—and any other

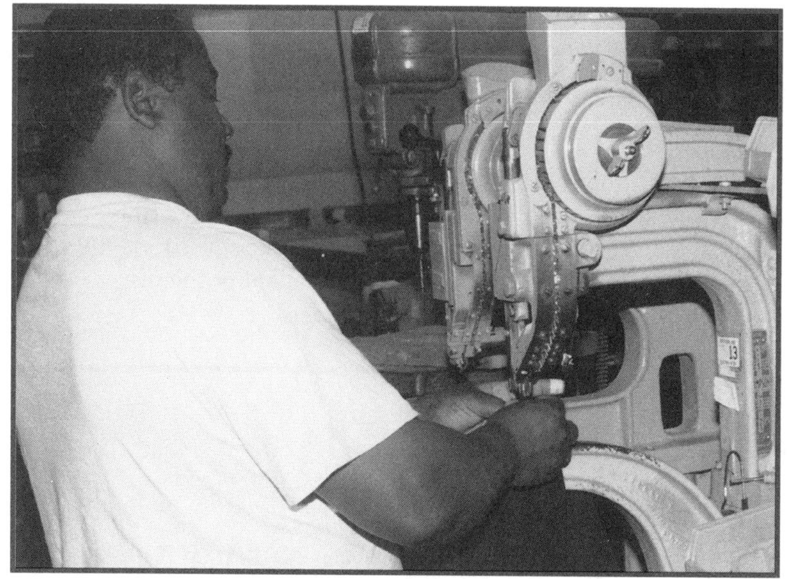

The CNC sponsors employment and training programs throughout the Cuban community of Miami. This man is learning to use a machine that will help him find a job in industry.

refugees—out of Cuba. Those in Cuba who could rent or build crafts were also allowed to go.

Suddenly, the Straits of Florida were crowded with boats of every description going to or coming from Cuba. Within about 6 months, more than 125,000 Marielitos, as the new refugees were called, landed in the United States. The arrival of this large wave of refugees marked a turning point in the Cuban American community. Among the Marielitos were large numbers of Cubans of African origin, who were from the poor, less educated classes in Cuba. It was impossible to find housing for all the refugees, and many lived along the streets of Little Havana.

The Mariel boatlift also caused problems in the Cuban American community and the surrounding area for another reason. Before opening the port of Mariel, Castro had ordered Cuba's prisons and mental hospitals to free large numbers of inmates. Those people were transported to Mariel, and many of them made their way into the United States.

The sudden appearance of the Marielitos served to heighten the tension between the Cuban American and white communities in Miami. Voters approved a law that year to overturn Dade county's bilingual policies. Miami's Cuban Americans felt caught in the middle during the months following the boatlift. On one hand, most members of the Cuban American community felt that their hard work had earned them an equal status in the city. On the other hand, absorbing enormous numbers of new immigrants—some of whom were criminals or mentally unstable people—asked a great deal of the residents of Little Havana.

Building for Success

The arrival of a new wave of Cuban immigrants coupled with the growing populations of non-Cuban Hispanic residents pushed the CNC into action during the 1980s. The most immediate need was that of low-income housing. The task of providing such housing began with zoning applications and ended when actual construction started. Accomplishing such a feat required up to 2 years.

Today, the CNC owns and manages 10 buildings of 100 apartments each. These award-winning complexes for low-income senior citizens, called the Echo Housing Project, house elderly individuals in units that are next to units occupied by family, relatives, or friends.

But housing was only one aspect of the CNC's community service. To answer the needs of a large group of teenagers who were at risk of dropping out of school, the Council founded educational programs such as the Little Havana Institute. These schools work in small groups to make certain that each student's academic goals are met.

Next to be started were programs for low-income members of the community. The CNC sponsored vocational retraining for older workers whose job skills were no longer needed. CNC also offers training for long-term unemployed immigrants and GED programs. Job training includes both helping them earn college degrees and training in such vocations as nurses, air conditioner technicians, auto mechanics, and computer programmers.

In 1984, the CNC started the Hispanic Leadership Training Program to educate young adults in community issues. Through this program, the CNC hopes it can increase the participation of Hispanics in the county. In the Hispanic Leadership Training Program, participants attend five sessions and learn from panels of government officials, newspaper specialists, fund-raising experts, and local leaders.

As the 1980s ended, Cuba's chief supporter, the Soviet Union, fell apart, and communism was recognized for its failure. The breakup of the Soviet Union brought economic ruin to Cuba and resulted in the most recent wave of *balseros* in 1994. By that time, the Hispanic presence in Miami was well established, and organizations such as the CNC and other private assistance agencies were able to respond effectively.

Through the work of the first "golden exiles", the next generation of ABC's (American-Born Cubans), and such organizations as the CNC, the Cuban American community has become an important part of the United States. Although the story of one person, such as Federico Sealy, is satisfying, it is only one of thousands that highlight the contributions of Cuban Americans. Through their struggles and successes, their family loyalty and hard work, these newcomers to the United States have followed the same pattern as others who have come in search of new beginnings.

Active Learning: Imagine that you are now a volunteer worker for the CNC. Your task is to provide job training for recent immigrants. Again, there are different levels of needs. List the steps that you would take to prepare recent immigrants for obtaining a job.

Thinking It Over

1. What problems did the Mariel boatlift cause in the Cuban American community?
2. **Making Inferences** How might life in the Cuban American community have been different if the CNC had not existed?

Through its Hispanic Leadership Training Program, the CNC teaches people how to take active roles in their neighborhoods. Many of these people will become members of committees and commissions in improving their communities.

Going to the Source

The Bilingual Debate

Currently, about 7 percent of all students in public schools do not understand English; however, the percentage is higher in some states. Bilingual education—teaching students in their native language and in English—is a controversial subject in many places. In several states, some people are demanding that all students in public schools be taught primarily in English unless their parents request otherwise. They argue that children who don't speak English should be required to learn the language. Many native-born Americans support the English-only movement, as do many immigrants who see learning English as a key to success in this country. However, some immigrant groups support the continuation of bilingualism as an effort to preserve immigrant culture and to promote political power.

The following section is from America's English Need Not Divide or Censor, a pamphlet published by the Cuban American Council. Read the passage, then answer the questions below based on information in both the section and in the case study.

> *English-only laws will move us further along the path of monolingualism—precisely at a time when we should be developing and preserving the valuable language resources our immigrant populations bring with them.*
>
> *English is not threatened. Then why threaten those who have come to these shores to adopt and contribute to our democracy and our economic system?*

1. How does the CNC feel about English-only laws?
2. What is "monolingualism"?
3. **Inference** What are the "valuable language resources our immigrant populations bring with them" as mentioned in the section?
4. **Inference** How might English-only laws threaten immigrants from non-English speaking countries?
5. **Developing an Opinion** Do you think that immigrants to the United States should have to learn English? Why or why not?

Case Study Review

Identifying Main Ideas

1. How did the people's attitudes toward Fidel Castro change between the time he entered Havana until he declared his form of government?
2. How were the first Cuban refugees after Castro took control treated differently from other immigrant groups? Why were they treated differently?
3. Why did the need for community organizations such as the CNC arise as the Cuban American population began to grow?

Working Together

Form a group with three classmates. Review this case study and choose one member of the group to represent each of the waves of Cuban refugees—the "golden exiles", the *balseros*, and the Marielitos. Have each person write a "biography" about the kind of person that might have been in each group of refugees. Use your school, local library, or the Internet for additional resources.

Active Learning

Create a Service Organization Review the lists of needs that you have prepared throughout the case study. Choose a specific group (the homeless, immigrants, teens, elderly, the jobless, etc.) in your community that might benefit from an agency that addressed those needs. Create an outline of steps that you would take to address the immediate, intermediate, and long term needs of that group. Write out a narrative action plan for your agency.

Lessons for Today

Although Cubans established a strong community and met with great success in Miami, some other communities resented the special treatment that Cubans received. African Americans in the 1960s, who were struggling for equality, sometimes said that political refugees from Cuba received better treatment in Florida than African American citizens. How might the opportunity given to people change with their race or national origin? Write a brief essay explaining your point of view on the importance of education in being able to take advantage of opportunities.

What Might You Have Done?

It is 1960, and you have just married. Your family's store has been taken over by Castro's government. Your parents believe that communism will ruin Cuba and want to leave for the United States. You are afraid—you do not want to leave your friends and your home. You do not know anything about America, and you don't speak English. You don't think Castro will stay in power for very long. What would you do? Why?

CRITICAL THINKING

Drawing Conclusions

Base Judgments on Evidence

Has anyone ever said to you, "Don't jump to conclusions"? That person is telling you not to make a judgment or form an opinion about something without adequate evidence. Critical thinkers look for evidence, or clues, in the information they read. They relate the evidence to their own experiences in order to draw an informed opinion.

The primary source below is a section of an article about the U.S. Census Bureau's report on the foreign-born population that appeared in the CNC newsletter. Read the information, then answer the questions based on this primary source and information in the case study.

> *Recent arrivals among the foreign-born are more likely to live in poverty, to have lower incomes, and to have higher unemployment rates than the native born. However, foreign-born people who have been here more than 6 years seem to have recovered from their initial [first] economic hardship. In fact, those who arrived during the 1970s are doing as well as natives in terms of earning their income.*
>
> *Foreign-born persons were more likely to receive Aid to Families with Dependent Children, Supplemental Security Income, or general welfare payments (5.8%) when compared to natives. However, the rates of these types of government assistance decline significantly as length of residency in America increases. In fact, welfare rates of immigrants who have been here 15 years or more are no different than those of persons born in the United States.*

1. What happens to immigrants as their length of stay in the United States increases?
2. How was Havana different from many other cities in the United States?
3. About how long does it take immigrants to reach the economic level of native-born citizens?
4. **Drawing Conclusions** Would you agree with this statement: If you give immigrants a chance, they will earn their way just like other Americans? Explain your answer.

Thousands of immigrants attend naturalization ceremonies each month. They have met all the qualifications for citizenship, including a five-year waiting period.

CASE STUDY 8

ACHIEVING THE AMERICAN DREAM

CRITICAL QUESTIONS

- Why do so many immigrants decide to become U.S. citizens?
- What accomplishment do the immigrants in this case study have in common?

TERMS TO KNOW

- naturalization
- refugees
- sponsors
- persecution
- pogroms

ACTIVE LEARNING

In this case study, you will read about the success stories of four immigrants who made new lives for themselves in the United States. At the end of the case study, you will choose one of the people you have read about. Then you will work with a partner to role-play an interview with that person. As you read, look for the Active Learning boxes to help you with your assignment.

On a mid-September morning in a small Connecticut courtroom, a crowd of people stand shoulder to shoulder, their right hands raised in the air. They come from all over the world: Asia, Africa, Central America, and Europe. But they all have one thing in common—their decision to become U.S. citizens.

Individually, they have each met the requirements for **naturalization**, the process by which individuals who are born in one nation become citizens of another. Now, together in a formal ceremony, they recite the words that will change their lives forever. With proud, happy faces, these immigrants—representing more than 70 different countries—pledge the Oath of Allegiance to the United States of America.

This same scene takes place month after month in courtrooms throughout the country. Requests for U.S. citizenship are at an all time high, having increased from about 200,000 in 1991 to more than 1.5 million in 1997.

Naturalized citizens enjoy the same rights and privileges as U.S.-born citizens, such as freedom of speech, freedom of religion, the right to vote, and the protection of U.S. laws. Often, immigrants who become citizens have decided that the United States offers them more rights, more chances for success, and more opportunities to become involved in government than their homelands.

Most come to this country eager to pursue their version of the "American Dream"—and many have succeeded.

But success doesn't necessarily mean a big paycheck. It can also mean a steady job, a warm home, and food on the table. For some, it means sending their children to college or making a difference in their community. There are many ideas about what it means to be successful, and those ideas are as different as the people who pursue them.

A Good Book to Read

Shadow of the Dragon by Sherry Garland. New York: Harcourt Brace, 1993.

Vietnamese refugee Danny Vo came to the United States as a young child. Now 16, he struggles with the conflict between his traditional Vietnamese home life and his new American way of life. This book provides a moving story of the immigrant experience.

A Good Movie to See

Selena. 1997 (128 minutes)

This feature film tells the tragic but inspiring story of Selena, a young Mexican-American girl who, with the support of her family, achieved great musical success. The film highlights togetherness as an important value in Mexican-American families. It also reveals the struggle Mexican Americans face when trying to balance their Mexican heritage with their American heritage, an experience to which many immigrants can relate.

1 Living Off the Sea

Tuong Cao, a Vietnamese immigrant, worked hard to build a life for his family in the United States. A shrimper, Cao spends weeks at a time aboard his fishing boat, a few miles off the Texas shore in the Gulf of Mexico. Cao comments,

> *From the time we leave the dock, the engine never stops. It's go, go, go, until we come back. Then we go out again.*

But Cao doesn't complain. He supports his family, enjoys his work, and likes being his own boss. He and his family have come a long way since they first set foot in the United States more than 20 years ago as **refugees**, people who fled from their home country to find safety in another.

Fleeing His Homeland

From his early teens into his twenties, Cao had fished with his father along the coast of South Vietnam from dawn to dusk almost every day, catching shrimp and finfish in large nets. But the Vietnam War changed all that.

For many years, Vietnam had been divided into two parts: North Vietnam, which had a communist government, and South Vietnam with its noncommunist government. Each side wanted to control the country. Eventually the two sides went to war. The United States joined in to help South Vietnam fight communism. But in 1973, after the North and South agreed to stop fighting, U.S. troops began to leave. When fighting broke out again, the North won and, in 1975, its communist government took over the entire country.

Cao fought as a soldier in the South Vietnamese Marines, while his family members watched the war destroy their beautiful country. Cao's family worried that when the war ended, its fishing boat would be confiscated. The communist government took over thousands of private businesses and forced many people to take new jobs. Many South Vietnamese believed the communists would also kill their former enemies. Cao's family members decided that, for their own safety, they would have to leave the country.

As soon as Cao's military service ended, he, his parents, his wife, and many of their neighbors crowded into his family's fishing boat and made their way out to sea, bringing whatever food and drinking water they could carry. They were among hundreds of thousands of Vietnamese—known as "boat people"— who left the country in this way.

Their trip was a dangerous one. As Cao explains,

> *A lot of people were seasick and were vomiting all the time. We were afraid we wouldn't make it—afraid we would run out of water and food, that we might sink, or the motor might break down.*

Such things happened frequently to boat people. Thousands became sick and died when their food and water supplies ran out. Others drowned in the South China Sea when their overcrowded boats sank. Some were captured by Vietnamese sea patrols and were returned to Vietnam. Those who survived were often attacked by sea pirates before finally arriving at refugee camps in Malaysia, Indonesia, or Thailand.

Cao's family was lucky. After only three days at sea, a U.S. ship rescued them and brought them to safety.

Many Vietnamese fishermen, such as Tuong Cao, settled in states along the Gulf Coast. Determined to succeed in the fishing business, they bought secondhand equipment or made their own. Cao repairs his nets over and over each winter to be ready for the spring fishing season.

Fishing can be a lonely business. From dawn to dusk during shrimp season, Tuong Cao is out on his boat, making a living just as his ancestors did in Vietnam. He says his children will not follow him into the fishing trade.

A Difficult Beginning

Vietnamese refugees went to many countries around the world, including Australia, Canada, China, and France. But the United States took in more than all the other countries combined.

In 1975 alone, about 150,000 Vietnamese refugees came to the United States. By 1985, more than 260,000 had arrived. With the help of **sponsors**, people or organizations who agree to help refugees find jobs and housing, large numbers of Vietnamese refugees went to California and Texas, as well as to other states around the country.

Cao's sponsor brought him, his wife, and their young son to a small southwestern town, where Cao found work in a shoe repair shop and began to learn English. It took a while to adjust to life in the United States. The traditions, language, foods, occupations, and values differed greatly from what the family had known in Vietnam. Vietnamese also faced rejection and sometimes violence from Americans who feared competition for jobs or who felt racial prejudice against Vietnamese people.

For Cao, the biggest problems came when he built a boat and started his own fishing business after working hard for 11 years and saving his money. By then he had six sons and had moved his family to the Gulf Coast near New Orleans.

Native-born fishers, who already lived along the coast, resented having Vietnamese refugees move in on what they considered to be their territory. In some areas, that resentment led to violence. Angry mobs vandalized Vietnamese shrimping boats and sometimes set them on fire. One newspaper reported an anti-Vietnamese rally in Galveston Bay, Texas, by the Ku Klux Klan. Says Cao,

> *We work day and night, then we come in and sell a lot of shrimp, and people get mad at us. We are catching more shrimp than the Americans and they don't like it.*

That was certainly true. But the problem also resulted from the fact that Cao and other Vietnamese fishers were unaware of U.S. fishing laws that restricted fishing territories and net size. In Vietnam, they had worked without restrictions, so when they worked in the United States with oversized nets and in areas that were off limits, the native fishers became angry. Once the Vietnamese fishers understood and obeyed the written and unwritten rules of shrimping, they were able to resolve most of their problems.

Hard Work Brings Rewards

Today, Cao continues to do what he knows best—work hard. Even in winter, when shrimp are out of season, he keeps busy. Day after day, from morning until evening, he repairs his nets and prepares his boat and equipment for the spring shrimp season.

After more than 20 years in the United States, Cao is not rich, but his family members are settled and well cared for. They have adopted a new language and a new way of life. Although Cao holds on to many Vietnamese customs and values, some traditions have changed. Cao says his sons will not follow him into the fishing trade, as he followed his own father. He has bigger plans for them—and those plans have nothing to do with the sea.

Cao's oldest son already attends college, and the others, whose ages range from 10 to 19, go to local schools. He hopes that they will all one day move into professional careers, which he says would be his greatest reward.

Thinking It Over

1. What dangers did Tuong Cao and his family risk by taking their crowded boat into the South China Sea?
2. **Drawing Conclusions** What might both local fishers and Vietnamese fishers have done to ease the tensions between the two groups?

2 A Community Leader

Daniella Henry found success by helping others to be successful. A Haitian immigrant, Henry is the director of the Haitian American Community Council (HACC) in Delray Beach, Florida. HACC provides services and aid for other Haitian immigrants.

Haitians have immigrated to the United States for hundreds of years, although the largest groups have come during times of political change and revolution in Haiti. Between 1915 and the late 1960s, government **persecution**, or cruel treatment that results in suffering, caused many Haitians to seek safety in the United States. Mostly well-educated men and women, they had little trouble finding work or setting up their own businesses in cities such as Chicago, Miami, New Orleans, and New York.

Today, Haitians continue to flee their homeland, but they do so mainly to escape extreme poverty. Since the early 1970s, the majority of Haitians have come in search of work and a chance to educate their children. Many hope to send money home to help family members still living in Haiti. They are mostly poor and poorly educated, and they need help adjusting to life in the United States. That's where Daniella Henry comes in.

The Early Years

Henry understands the challenges of settling in a foreign country. She was 16 when she joined her mother in the United States—and she did not speak English.

Like many Haitian immigrants, Henry's mother had come in search of work. "She came for work because she was a single mother of five and she needed a job to support us," says Henry. "First she came to settle, and then she brought us here later."

Henry's mother came in 1972 and sent for her children in 1975. The family settled in Miami, Florida. At the time, there were few Haitians in her community. She remembers being teased by other children for being different. As she recalls,

> *The other students—we were just like aliens to them. Because that was the first time they were seeing some Haitian children, so they didn't know how to behave themselves. We were getting tortured by them.*

In recent years, Florida's Haitian population has grown significantly. Large numbers of Haitians have also settled in New York, Chicago, Miami, New Orleans, Washington, D.C., and Boston. In these cities, Haitians find work cleaning homes, caring for children, and working in hotels, and they have started their own Haitian-run restaurants, groceries, record stores, and other family businesses, as well as cultural organizations.

Active Learning: Think about whether you would like to interview Tuong Cao or Daniella Henry. Prepare three or four questions about either person's experience.

Soon after Daniella Henry moved to the Miami area, she realized that Haitian immigrants needed a spokesperson to help them stand up for their rights. Here, she counsels several immigrants as a radio station broadcasts the discussion.

Although Henry had moved away from Florida as an adult, the growth of its Haitian community eventually lured her back—but it was to be a long journey.

A Turn for the Worse

After completing high school in Florida, Henry moved to Washington, D.C., to attend college. Upon graduating, she accepted a job offer and moved again—to New York City. It seemed as if she was finally on the road to success.

But things soon took a turn for the worse. After working in New York for a while, Henry became pregnant. She gave birth three months before her baby was due. Her tiny, premature son remained hospitalized for many weeks. Once released, he had to be taken for therapy treatments and medical appointments. A single mother, Henry felt she had no choice but to quit her job and apply for government money to help support her family and pay her baby's enormous medical bills. She says,

> *I couldn't go to work any more, because I had to stay home to take him to therapy. There was no way that I could go to work and take him to different appointments at the same time. I had nowhere to turn and went temporarily on welfare to help me out.*

Henry admits it was painful, but she feels she made the right decision. "Being a single mother and having a sick child in the hospital, it was so much demand on me," she says. Still, she was determined to work her way back up. Her road to success, it turned out, was by helping others like herself.

Working Her Way Up

Henry began by counseling other mothers on public assistance at a local community center. Eventually, she worked her way up and no longer needed government money. She discovered that she had a gift for helping people and, what's more, she enjoyed it.

In the early 1990s, Henry decided to take her newly discovered talent and move back to Florida. Like many Haitians living in the North, she had heard much about Florida's expanding Haitian community, especially in Palm Beach County. It had become the number-one spot for recently arrived Haitians, growing from just over 10,000 in 1990 to more than 60,000 in 1997. She recalls,

> *When I first came to Delray Beach, they really needed somebody, because the [Haitian] population was growing and there was nobody to stand up for them. There were so many needs. I came at the right time.*

Fleeing desperate poverty and an unstable government, Haitians came to the United States as refugees seeking safety. Henry arrived just as hundreds of Haitian refugees "started pouring onto the shores of Florida." Immediately, she became involved in the refugee settlement program, helping refugees find jobs and homes, translating their immigration papers, and helping them adjust to life in the United States. She explains,

> *We were kind of a guidance place for them. Where they would come for services to get adjusted to the country.*

Making a Difference

Through her work with the Haitian American Community Council, Henry continues to provide services to Haitian immigrants—to newcomers and those who have lived in the United States for a while. In addition, the council offers parenting classes for adults and after-school programs for children. Henry says,

> *The component of parenting is very important. There's a big difference between raising kids in Haiti and raising them here. In Haiti, they believe in spanking a lot. Here, it's [considered] abuse.*

Henry says that parenting classes show Haitian parents how to raise their children without hitting them or spanking them severely. The after-school programs help Haitian children build their self-esteem, their self-confidence, and a sense of cultural pride.

Henry hopes the classes HACC offers will help Haitian immigrants overcome the barriers to happiness in their new country and set them on the road to achieving their own measure of success.

Thinking It Over

1. Why do Haitians flee their country?
2. **Analyzing** In what way does Daniella Henry consider her life in the United States to be a success?

Having arrived from Haiti as a teenager, Daniella Henry understands the challenges of settling into a new country. She directs the Haitian American Community Council, a service organization for Haitian immigrants.

3 For the Love of Music

When Ilya Rutman, a Russian Jewish immigrant, first thought about coming to the United States in 1989, he was scared. "In school, we were taught America was cement houses, smoke and no trees, people living under bridges," he says. But he knew that if he wanted to improve his life, he would have to go. As a Jew, his life in Russia was oppressive.

Like many Russian Jews, Rutman was treated unfairly. Growing up, he had been harassed, especially by classmates. As he recalls,

When I was in school, I got beat up real bad. I said, "Why?" The kids said, "Because you are a Jew." That happened in 1967, and it never goes away.

Escape From Persecution

Rutman's professional life also suffered. A talented musician, Rutman began playing the violin at age 13. "I already knew I wanted to become a violinist," he recalled. "I love violin, I love playing violin." By the time he was 25, he held a position with the Symphony Orchestra, and six years later he joined the Moldavian Folk Music Orchestra. Still, he could go only so far. He says,

The whole orchestra could travel. I couldn't. The conductor sends the list to the KGB, and they say yes or no. It was always no. It was constantly, "He's a Jew." I was carrying this stamp.

Russian Jews have been persecuted in their country for centuries. They began coming to the United States in large numbers in the 1880s, when a new government with strong anti-Jewish feelings came into power. Under this government, **pogroms**, or government-sponsored violent raids on Jewish communities, occurred frequently. Thousands of Jews were killed, and their shops and synagogues destroyed. By 1914, one third of all Jews in Russia had emigrated, most of them to the United States.

During those years, many of the Jews who left Russia had to sneak across the border and make their way to a foreign seaport. However, in the 1970s, Russia changed its policy, giving Jews more freedom to leave the country. As a result, 110,000 Jews left Russia during the 1970s. About 15,000 of them came to the United States, and more than half settled in New York City.

Starting Out

Rutman's brother had emigrated to the United States ten years earlier, and he convinced Rutman that he would have more opportunities there. So, in 1989, Rutman arrived in New York City with his wife and children, a few belongings, and less than $500 in his pocket. He recalls,

I was scared. We came here with $120 per person and luggage filled with pillows, blankets, winter clothes, and frying pans—that was our luggage. We weren't afraid of a hard job, just a lack of job. We just wanted a decent life.

Jewish Vocational Services, an organization that helps Jewish immigrants, came to the aid of Rutman and his family, helping him to find housing and a job. Rutman quickly found a

After arriving in the United States with only $500, Ilya Rutman now has a successful business. Still, his real love is playing the violin. "The first time I stepped into a violin shop," he says, "that was it."

position with a piano shop in Connecticut where he worked for almost a year. Then, he heard about a job at a piano shop in Boston and moved his family there. He hoped to use the opportunity to attend a violin-making course being offered in the area; making violins was something he had wanted to do since childhood.

However, after Rutman arrived in Boston, the job fell through. He searched desperately for work, going to pizza places, gas stations, and other businesses, before finally giving up and applying for government money. He says,

> *I felt really embarrassed. I thought, "I am healthy, I must work." To go on welfare and have other people work and get taxed, that was my worst experience.*

Rutman finally found work delivering pizzas. Later that year, he enrolled in a violin-making course and earned money by tuning pianos at night.

Active Learning: What would you ask if you interviewed Ilya Rutman? Add two or three questions to your notes.

A Thriving Business

Finally, in 1993, Rutman returned to the work he loves best. With a loan from Jewish Vocational Services, he opened Rutman's Musical Workshop, a now thriving business that services and restores pianos, grand pianos, violins, violas, and cellos. In the early years, he also taught violin, but he doesn't any longer. "I'm too tough of a teacher," he says. "I require too much."

In 1995, two Boston-area newspapers wrote articles about Rutman. He says his customers appreciated seeing the articles and called him to offer their congratulations. "It assures that I provide a quality job," he says. "It works like word of mouth. It will bring recognition as a specialist."

Rutman's business success has led to other successes for his family—since moving to Boston, Rutman has played professional violin with the New England Conservatory of Music, and his wife recently received her nursing degree. His children, he says, are getting a better education in the United States than they ever could in Russia.

Although Rutman is not yet a United States citizen, he plans to begin the naturalization process soon. He is grateful for the opportunities this country has given him and for the people who helped him achieve his dream. He says,

> *This is a payoff country. The more you invest, the more you get back. I'm not greedy. If I can pay the mortgage and put bread on the table, it's enough.*

Thinking It Over

1. How did the Russian government treat Jews?
2. **Making Comparisons** What opportunities did Ilya Rutman have in the United States that he did not have in Russia?

4 Tortillas by the Ton

Fernando Sanchez is another immigrant with a thriving business. A Mexican immigrant, Sanchez opened Tortilleria Piaxtla, Inc., the first tortilla factory in Brooklyn, New York, in 1986. Together with four other tortilla shops that have opened since then, Tortilleria Piaxtla serves New York's large Mexican community—which by the summer of 1994, had reached over 100,000 people.

Altogether, more than 17 million Mexicans live in the United States, and their population continues to grow. Most Mexicans settle in the border states—California, Texas, New Mexico, Arizona, and Colorado. But communities are also growing in other states, such as New York, New Jersey, Oklahoma, Oregon, Pennsylvania, and Washington State. Mexicans are the largest and fastest growing foreign-born ethnic group in the United States.

Heading North

Most Mexicans come to the United States in search of work. The Mexican economy is poor, and the unemployment rate is high—at times, up to half of the people are out of work. Often, jobs in Mexico pay only a few cents an hour, and very few pay as well as even the least popular jobs in the United States. By coming to the United States, Mexicans can make up to six times more money than if they stayed there. In addition, many Mexicans sometimes start their own businesses here or have the skills and education to get better-paying jobs.

Step by Step

Fernando Sanchez came to the United States in 1969 with no skills and no money. He joined his brother Enrique, who had arrived a year before. During their first few years, the brothers worked as dishwashers, then as cooks, and finally as chef's assistants in New York restaurants. Along the way, they learned both English and a great deal about running a business. They also saved enough money to bring two other brothers and Fernando's wife to the United States.

By 1986, Fernando had saved $10,000 and decided it was time to start his own business. He bought a used tortilla press, rented space in an abandoned garage, and went to work, naming his company after his hometown in Mexico.

At first, Fernando's business was not successful. It didn't help that his shop was located in a dangerously run down neighborhood. "When we started here, every night someone was robbed leaving my place," he recalls. But before long, the neighborhood filled with new families arriving from Mexico, and as the community grew, crime decreased—and his profits increased.

By 1992, Fernando was doing well enough to buy the garage he had been renting. The year after that he expanded into the space next door and built a factory outlet store, Plaza Piaxtla, across the street.

Active Learning: What would you want to know about Fernando Sanchez's experience? Add two or three questions to your notes.

Just 10 years ago, few tortilla factories existed on the East Coast. Now there is a growing interest in traditional Mexican foods. To meet the demand, Enrique Sanchez's tortilla shop in Rhode Island delivers to cities in New York, New Jersey, and Connecticut.

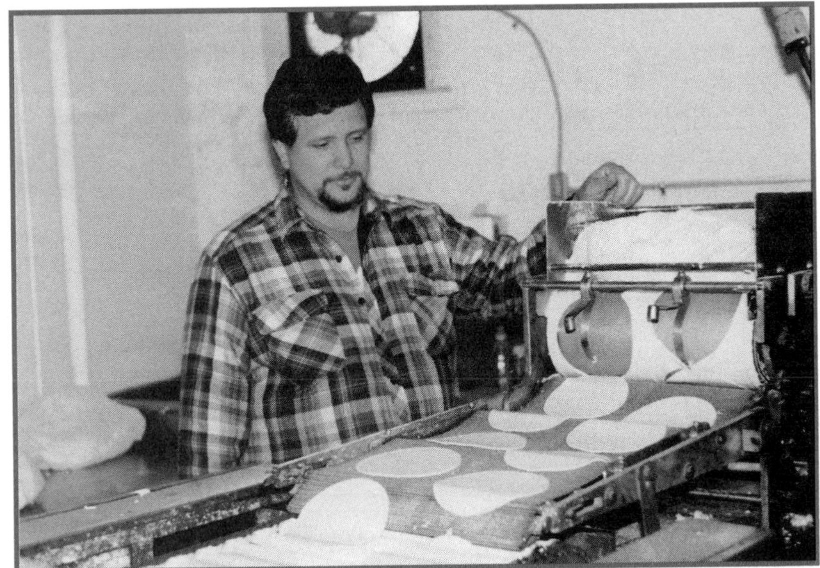

Enrique Sanchez and his brother Fernando worked at many odd jobs before opening a business to meet the needs of New York's Mexican community. Here, Enrique operates a tortilla pressing machine.

The Taste of Success

In his first year, Fernando produced 4,000 tortillas a week. By 1992, his weekly count had reached 400,000, a total that required over 200 tons of corn flour per month. As he says,

> *A typical Mexican family, mama and papa and four kids, goes through two or three packages of my tortillas every time they sit down to eat.*

Today, Tortilleria Piaxtla, Inc. has over $4 million in annual sales, a chain of Brooklyn bakeries, a grocery store, and a tortilla shop in Providence, Rhode Island, which is operated by Enrique and his son. Beginning with just two workers in 1986, Fernando now employs as many as 50, mostly immigrants like himself. His trucks deliver tortillas to cities in New York, New Jersey, Connecticut, and Pennsylvania. He even ships his products as far away as Canada.

Besides helping himself, Fernando has helped other Mexicans succeed as well, either by loaning them money for their passage to the United States or by helping them start their own tortilleria shops. He says that he's not worried about the competition. Fernando says that the Latino population is growing so steadily that there are more than enough customers to go around.

A Land of Opportunity

When many immigrants like Tuong Cao, Daniella Henry, Ilya Rutman, and Enrique Sanchez come to the United States, they bring with them energy and a determination to succeed. For them and the thousands like them, the United States continues to be a land of opportunity, offering hope, education, and a possibility of success not available to them in their homelands. While many native-born Americans take their citizenship for granted, immigrants seeking its freedoms and protections know firsthand what makes U.S. citizenship special.

Thinking It Over

1. What do Mexicans like Fernando Sanchez hope to find in the United States?
2. **Making Inferences** What need did Fernando Sanchez meet in his community?

GOING TO THE SOURCE

Becoming a United States Citizen

Immigrants must meet many requirements before they can take the oath of citizenship. Among other things, they must be at least 18 years old, understand English, and have some knowledge of U.S. history and of how the government works. They must also wait five years after officially declaring their wish to become citizens, during which time they must live in the United States. Below are 15 of the 100 questions on the citizenship test given by the Immigration and Naturalization Service (INS). Read the INS-test questions and then answer the questions that follow.

INS-Test Questions

5. Who said "Give me liberty or give me death"?
9. What country did we fight during the Revolutionary War?
16. In what year was the Constitution written?
29. What did the Emancipation Proclamation do?
32. How many states are there in the United States?
35. Name one purpose of the United Nations.
38. What is the supreme law of the United States?
42. What are the three branches of our government?
46. Name one right guaranteed by the First Amendment.
55. Where does Congress meet?
64. Can you name two U.S. Senators from your state?
79. How many terms can a President serve?
86. What are the duties of the Supreme Court?
91. What is the capital of your state?
98. What is the most important right granted to U.S. citizens?

1. How long is the waiting period after a person applies to become a U.S. citizen?
2. **Drawing Conclusions** Why do you think it's important for U.S. citizens to know how their government works?
3. **Making Inferences** Based on the questions you see here, how do you think immigrants might prepare for this test?

Case Study Review

Identifying Main Ideas

1. What does it mean to become "naturalized"?
2. Why did the people in this case study decide to leave their native lands?
3. What characteristics do the people in this case study have in common?
4. How has each person achieved success in the United States?

Working Together

Work together with three or four classmates to draw an Immigrant Success Stories chart. Draw five columns and four rows on the chart. At the top of the chart write the headings: Name; Homeland; Reasons for Coming; Problems Overcome; and Achievements. In the rows beneath the first heading, list the names of the persons you read about in this case study. Then review the case study and use information about each person to fill in the remaining rows.

Active Learning

Interviewing Choose a partner to work with. Together, review the notes you took as you read this case study. Choose a person from the case study to interview. Decide what questions you will ask that person. Then assign roles; one of you will be the interviewer, and the other will play the role of the immigrant being interviewed.

Lessons for Today

Two of the immigrants in this case study received government money to help them during a difficult time. Ilya Rutman needed help only a year after arriving in the United States. Today, new laws make it harder for non-citizens like Rutman to receive money from the U.S. government. Some people disagree with these laws. Others support them. What do you think? Should immigrants be allowed to apply for government money during their first few years in this country? Why or why not? Write a brief essay explaining your point of view.

What Might You Have Done?

Imagine that you are a Vietnamese fisher living in South Vietnam during the 1970's. The North Vietnamese government has just taken control of the country and is busy taking over all privately run businesses. You fear that yours will be next and that your family will be forced to give up a way of life it has known for generations. You consider using your boat to try to escape, but the trip would be dangerous. You know your family may not survive. What might you do? Write a short response describing your choice and your feelings about it.

CRITICAL THINKING

Using Comparison and Contrast

The Language of Thinking

Comparing is the process of finding similarities between two or more things. **Contrasting** is the process of finding differences. Critical thinkers know that sometimes situations that appear to be different prove to be similar in many ways. Other times, situations that seem to be alike turn out to be very different.

During the time that Daniella Henry was attending college in Washington, D.C., Ilya Rutman was playing professional violin in a Russian symphony orchestra. On the surface, the two appear to have little in common.

Daniella Henry came to the United States as a teenager to join her mother who had arrived a few years earlier. She went on to graduate from college and find a job in New York City. Ilya Rutman was married with two sons when he decided that his opportunities in Russia were limited. He made arrangements to leave his country, said good-bye to his friends, then flew by plane to the United States. Yet Henry and Rutman had a number of things in common. Use the information in the case study to answer the questions that follow.

- Why did Henry and Rutman leave their homelands?
- What memories do they have of their school years?
- What struggles did Henry and Rutman face in the United States?
- How did they overcome their difficulties?
- What qualities do Henry and Rutman share?
- What things do they value?

Below is a Venn diagram. It is used to help compare and contrast people and events. Copy the diagram into your notebook. In the overlapping parts of the circles, write down all the things that Henry and Rutman have in common. In the parts that do not overlap, write down what was unique about each person's experience. Write an essay comparing the two immigrants.

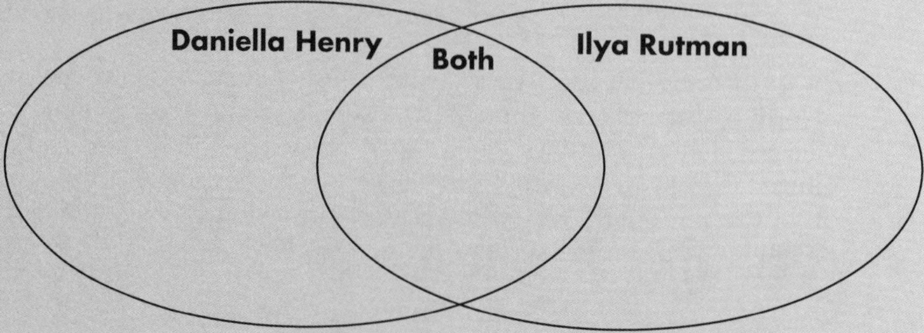

This exhibit at the Ellis Island Immigration Museum features many belongings that immigrants carried to the United States—handmade clothes, linens, musical instruments, and pictures of loved ones.

FOLLOW-UP

MANY VOICES, COMMON EXPERIENCES

CRITICAL QUESTIONS

- Should the continuing wave of immigrants entering the United States be controlled to a greater extent than it is now? Why or why not?
- What is the unconscious pattern that all immigrants seem to follow?

TERMS TO KNOW

- green cards
- humanitarian immigrants
- unauthorized immigrants
- amnesty

ACTIVE LEARNING

A mural is a large wall painting that depicts a scene. After you read this Follow-Up, you will create a sketch for a mural that symbolizes the immigrant experience. As you read, study the photos that you see and write down ideas to help you plan your mural.

Since 1820, about 60 million people have emigrated to the United States from many nations throughout the world. The United States is a country of immigrants—throughout U.S. history, people from all over the world have come seeking better lives. The image of the Statue of Liberty as a beacon of freedom and opportunity is an unforgettable sight for immigrants of the past as well as those who arrive today.

1 Changing Faces

Although the number of people entering the United States has risen in recent years, the system that exists for allowing immigrants into the country has changed little since 1965. In that year, Congress adopted an immigration law that took the place of one that had been in place for decades. The earlier system had used national origins as a basis for allowing people to enter the country. Under the old system, most immigrants entering the country came from Western European countries. The number of immigrants from Latin American, Asian, and African countries was limited.

Effects of the 1965 Immigration Act

When Congress passed the Immigration Act of 1965, the new law eliminated the national origin system of immigration. Instead, this act allowed immigrants already here to bring their relatives into the United States, and those people in turn could bring over more relatives.

This law limited immigration to 290,000 people annually and set general quotas for the entire Eastern and Western Hemispheres. It allowed immigrants from all over the world equal entry into the United States.

The law helped to change the racial mix of immigrants. Many new immigrants from Asia and Latin America entered the United States. But immigration from Europe dropped, mainly because during the 1960s, Communist governments refused to allow people to leave their countries.

The system remained unchanged until 1978, when a single worldwide quota was set. As a result of the changed immigration system, most of the approximately 800,000 immigrants who enter the United States each year come from eight countries—Mexico, the Philippines, Vietnam, the Dominican Republic, China, Taiwan, South Korea, and India.

A Different Outlook

As the change in the race of immigrants began during the 1970s, immigration became a concern for many Americans. Some felt that the rising tide of immigrants from non-European countries would change the racial mix of the United States, and by doing so, change the predominant white culture of the country.

For most of the 20th century, about 75 percent of the American population has been white. By the middle of the 21st century, experts estimate that about 50 percent of the U.S. population will be white, 14 percent will be black, 26 percent will

On the ground floor of the Ellis Island Immigration Museum, a platform is heaped with baskets, trunks, and suitcases. In this space, immigrants checked their baggage when they first arrived at Ellis Island.

be Hispanic, and 8 percent will be Asian. This makes some people uncomfortable or fearful.

Another factor in the changing attitude toward immigration has been the skill level of immigrants. In the past, immigrants could find work in industry in unskilled jobs—Slavic immigrants worked in coal mines and Jewish immigrants worked in the garment industry. Today, fewer jobs are available for unskilled workers. Thus, immigrants are competing with native-born citizens for a shrinking number of jobs that require lesser skills.

Of all the issues that have concerned Americans, providing government services for immigrants is one of the most debated. Many people wonder whether American taxpayers should pay for services to immigrants. For example, immigrants often require more government assistance than native-born Americans because their children need special help when learning English in public schools.

Although studies show that the average native-born family pays only about $50 overall in taxes per year to help immigrants, many Americans complain that immigrants are a burden. Those complaints have affected the attitudes of lawmakers in many areas of the country.

Active Learning: Think about the background colors you might use in a mural to illustrate the immigrant experience. What colors will illustrate hope? Which will illustrate despair?

Thinking It Over

1. Which groups of immigrants increased because of the Immigration Act of 1965?
2. **Making Inferences** What do you think was the effect of the Immigration Act of 1965 on the racial composition of the United States?

2 Open or Shut Gates

The following paragraphs are taken from "Stop the Unchecked Flood," an editorial that appeared in 1998 in an issue of the *Philadelphia Inquirer.*

> *As unfashionable as the term overpopulation is, we should give some thought to it. According to the Census Bureau, the United States could have 519 million people by 2050—some 20 million more than India had in 1965—within the lifetime of today's teenagers. Recent immigrants and their U.S.-born dependents will account for much of that future growth.*
>
> *So the questions become, Do we wish to leave our children in an overpopulated, heavily-indebted . . . America? We can keep letting high levels of immigration threaten the American standard of living. Or we can work to achieve an immigration policy in accordance with our national interests.*

This writer's opinion is that too many immigrants are coming into the United States. In recent years, once again, the debate over allowing immigrants into the United States has grown particularly sharp; so this opinion is not a surprise. However, the fact that the author was Yeh Ling-Ling, a Chinese immigrant to the United States, might be surprising to many people. It serves to put the question of who should enter the United States in a new perspective.

According to opinion polls, about two-thirds of Americans now believe that immigration should be restricted. Furthermore—as in the opinion of Yeh Ling-Ling—even those who themselves have emigrated to the United States are concerned about the number of newcomers arriving here.

Immigrants in the United States are classified in three ways. Legal immigrants are those who enter to join families or to work. They have **green cards**—permits that give them many of the same rights as American citizens, except for the right to vote. **Humanitarian immigrants** are those who enter as political refugees. **Unauthorized immigrants** are those who enter the country illegally or who remain in the U.S. after their visas have expired.

For those who favor restrictions on the number of immigrants entering the United States, certain figures may be a special cause for alarm. One figure might be 24 million—the approximate number of legal immigrants in the United States. These immigrants make up about 9.3 percent of the population.

Americans who favor restrictions might worry about the estimated 800,000 legal immigrants who have entered the United States each year since the 1980s. That number represents almost one-third of the growth in the U.S. population each year since 1980.

Whatever numbers are most critical to those who favor restrictions, they all add up to one fact. The United States is now experiencing the largest wave of immigration since the early 20th century—almost a million newcomers arrive each year.

Concerns About Immigration

As arguments about immigration continued during the 1980s, a new area of concern grew as well—illegal immigration. Experts estimate that about 300,000 people entered the United States illegally each year in the 1980s. Most came for jobs, and some employers hired illegal immigrants because they could be paid less than other workers and would not complain about working conditions.

In 1986, Congress passed the Immigration Reform and Control Act. This law attempted to curb illegal immigration by offering **amnesty**—a pardon—to illegal immigrants who had lived in the United States for 4 years and who had registered to become citizens.

The Immigration Act of 1990 increased the number of immigrants allowed into the United States by 40 percent—up to 675,000 immigrants per year. It also created separate categories such as "family-sponsored" and "work-sponsored" to allow a wider opening for immigrants to enter the country.

This law opened the gates for people around the world. Most new immigrants settled in the South and West and in large coastal cities such as San Francisco and New York. Those areas struggled to meet the immigrants' needs for education, jobs, and health services.

Immigration Controls

As native-born Americans in these areas and elsewhere struggled to compete for jobs, the addition of huge numbers of immigrants brought anti-immigrant feelings to the surface. In 1994, these feelings were expressed by voters in California who passed Proposition 187.

Proposition 187, which denied medical and education services to illegal immigrants, was

This exhibit at the Ellis Island Immigration Museum is called "The Word Tree." It shows that American English has borrowed words from the languages of the immigrants who have come here. Some of these words are "stampede" (Spanish) and "Yankee" (Dutch).

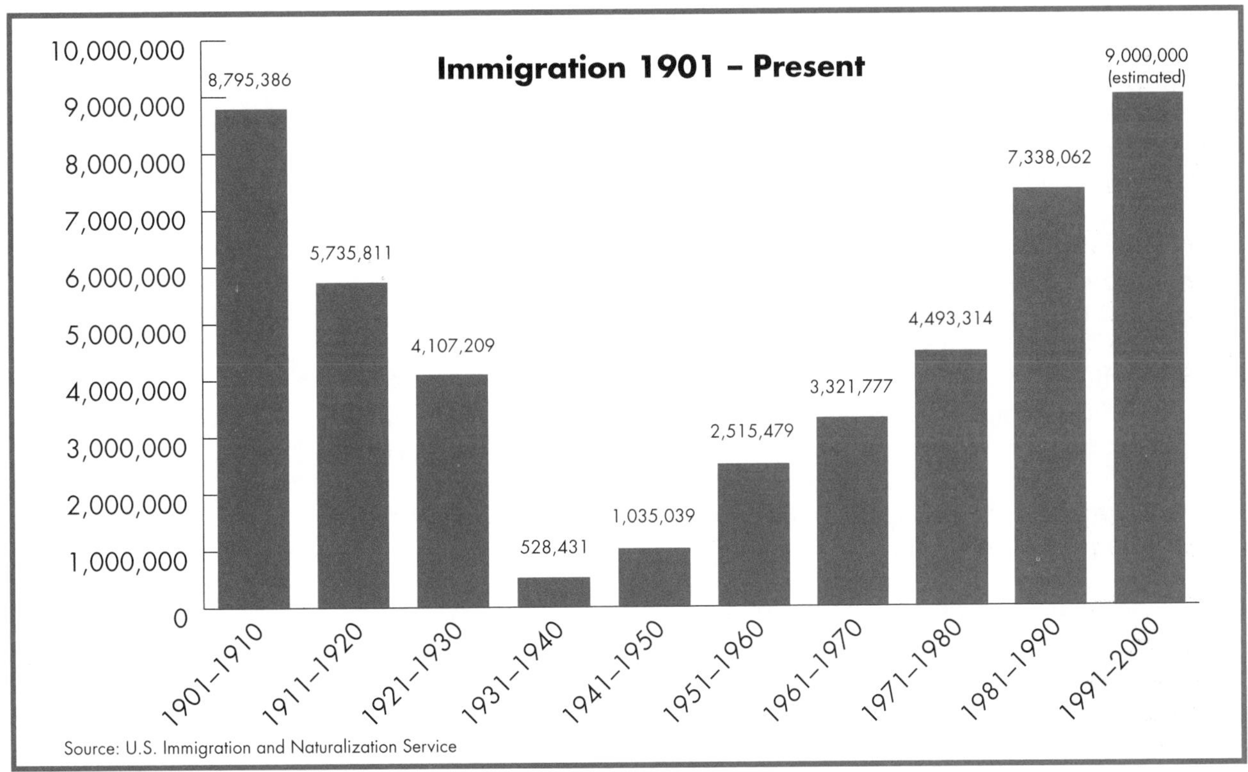

This bar graph shows immigration totals in ten-year periods. In which two periods were immigration numbers lowest? Why do you think immigration decreased during these two periods?

opposed by many Californians. For those people, the proposition represented a reaction against all immigrants. One newspaper editorial stated that

> *Proposition 187 forces public officials to deny vital services to anyone they SUSPECT might not be a legal resident. But Proposition 187 doesn't define the basis for such suspicion. Is it the way you speak? The sound of your last name? The shade of your skin?*

Although Proposition 187 was approved by a majority of California's voters, a judge declared it unconstitutional in 1998. The judge ruled that only the federal government has the power to regulate immigration. However, in many ways, the proposition drew a line between people who were pro-immigration and those who were anti-immigration.

Those who felt immigration must be more strictly controlled exerted their strength at the federal level in 1996 with the Welfare Reform Act. That law cut back food stamps and other federal benefits for immigrants and set a 5-year waiting period before immigrants could receive any benefits. The passage of the law resulted in the loss of benefits for many legal immigrants.

Besides congressional legislation, the U.S. government has taken other steps to limit immigration. In 1998, the United States changed the category for Cubans who leave their homeland from refugee to immigrant. This change allowed a smaller number of Cubans to enter the United States. The United States also agreed to return any Cubans who had left their country illegally.

A Tide of Immigrants

As the great flow of immigrants arrive on America's shores, the newcomers follow an unconscious pattern—a pattern that all immigrants seem to have in common and that has not changed much over the years. No matter which countries immigrants come from, newcomers tend to live near others who have arrived earlier from their country. They feel more at home sharing familiar clothing styles, foods, and customs in these communities. They develop their own businesses, places of worship, and other parts of their society to meet their needs.

Another part of the pattern concerns prejudice. When each new wave of immigrants arrives in large numbers, the people tend to face prejudice from native-born Americans. Some prejudice may be based on the ignorance and fear that comes out of an inability to accept a different way of life. Other prejudice is rooted in competition for jobs and housing. During times when the U.S. economy is not strong, prejudice becomes even more severe and often results in restrictive immigration policies.

For immigrants, the United States remains a shining beacon of freedom. Although they realize that it is not always the promised land, they also discover that they can achieve their dreams through hard work. For many immigrants, this means that they must give up some of the traditions of their homeland as family members—men and women—find work to buy what they need and want.

This exhibit, a mosaic of many faces of immigrants, is called "The American Flag." It demonstrates that the United States continues to be a magnet for people who seek freedom and opportunities.

Immigrants have made the United States a nation of diversity—they have brought their customs, their religions, their music, their festivals, their stories, and their language to the United States. Immigrants have also brought their knowledge and skills to benefit the United States. When the economies of local areas are strong, immigrants help to create jobs for everyone or take jobs that few native-born Americans want. Many work hard to make money to send to their families in their native lands.

Because over the years immigrants have brought their own cultures to the United States, they have helped all Americans to become more open about interpreting, understanding, and appreciating the many cultures of the world. By coming in contact with these other cultures, Americans have come to comprehend the many layers of their own culture—as a melting pot, a mosaic, and as a fantastic blend. As President John F. Kennedy said, "Everywhere immigrants have enriched and strengthened the fabric of American life."

As long as the United States maintains its position as the world's greatest economic power, immigrants will continue to seek entrance into the country. For some people, those who enter will gain the same chance that immigrants have always had—a chance to succeed, a chance to escape from persecution, a chance for a new beginning, a chance to become a contributing member of a democracy, a chance to live their dreams. For others, the continuing tide will change what it means to be an American.

Thinking It Over

1. How did the rising number of illegal immigrants cause problems for certain areas of the United States?
2. **Analyzing** Who might be the people who had the strongest feelings against Proposition 187?

Follow-Up Review

Identifying Main Ideas

1. How did the Immigration Act of 1965 change immigration patterns in the United States?
2. What do the different immigrant classifications such as legal, humanitarian, and unauthorized mean?
3. How did many people react as the immigration patterns changed in the United States?

Working Together

Work with two or three other students to design a monument in honor of immigration. Sketch a design for your monument and write a paragraph for a plaque to go on the monument. Then write a speech to give at the dedication of your group's monument. Present your design, plaque, and speech to your class.

Active Learning

Creating a Mural Work with two or three classmates to create a mural that reflects the changing immigration patterns as well as the changing perspective on immigration that you have read about in the Follow-Up. On a piece of paper, sketch your initial ideas for the mural. List the materials you will need in order to continue the project. Review your sketch and revise it, if needed. If possible, gather the materials and create your mural.

Lessons for Today

Immigrants have often been treated in prejudiced ways. What are some causes of discrimination against foreign-born people? Do you think it is difficult to unify a country in which people of different cultural backgrounds live? Do you think people in other countries have the same attitude? Write a newspaper editorial explaining your point of view on this subject.

What Might You Have Done?

Imagine that you are a lawmaker in the California legislature. You want to remain in office, and most of the voters in your district want you to vote for Proposition 187. You and your staff oppose it. How will you vote? How will you explain your vote?

GLOSSARY

amnesty a program through which illegal aliens could apply for U. S. citizenship if they could show proof of residency for five years (p. 49); a pardon (p. 120)

anarchists people who believe in a society without government or laws (p. 40)

assimilate to adapt to (p. 43)

balseros the Spanish term for rafters (p. 96)

bosses leaders of political machines (p. 71)

certificate of residence a special document that proved a Chinese immigrant was in the United States legally (p. 33)

Chinatowns Chinese neighborhoods (p. 33)

Chinese Exclusion Act a law that banned Chinese immigration for 10 years (p. 32)

confiscated took away (p. 66)

deported sent back (p. 17)

detained held up (p. 17)

discrimination unfair treatment (p. 41)

Ellis Island an immigration station near the Statue of Liberty (p. 12)

emigrated left one's native country to settle elsewhere (p. 56)

fongs social centers that ran clubs and provided opportunities for Chinese immigrants (p. 34)

Great Famine a famine in Ireland that took place in 1845 (p. 67)

green cards permits that give legal immigrants the same rights as American citizens, except for the right to vote (p. 119)

Harlem Renaissance a rebirth of artistic activity in Harlem (p. 59)

Homestead Act a law that allowed citizens and permanent immigrants to claim 160 acres of land for $10 (p. 24)

humanitarian immigrants immigrants who enter the U. S. as political refugees (p. 119)

immigrant a person who leaves one country to settle in another (p. 5)

indentured servants people who agreed to work for a certain number of years to pay off their passage to the United States (p. 68)

industrial revolution a rapid change in the production of goods from handmade to machine-made products (p. 81)

interned held prisoner (p. 46)

labor contractors people who hired extra workers in order to take on large assignments (p. 82)

literacy test a test given to immigrants to determine whether they could read (p. 44)

machines informal but powerful political organizations (p. 71)

manufactured produced with the help of machines and power tools (p. 81)

migrated moved (p. 57)

mosaic shapes of different colors joined together to make a larger pattern (p. 5)

mulattos people of mixed white and African heritage (p. 56)

nationalism loyalty to one's country (p. 44)

nativists people who felt that U. S. laws should favor native-born Americans (p. 41)

naturalization the process by which individuals who are born in one country become citizens of another (p. 104)

Pacific Railway Act a law that provided money for the transcontinental railroad (p. 25)

Penal Laws strict laws designed by the British to control the Irish (p. 66)

persecution cruel treatment (p. 107)

piecework process in which clothing manufacturers cut costs by dividing sewing tasks into small sections (p. 83)

political refugees people who flee from a country for political reasons (p. 95)

pogroms government-sponsored violent raids on Jewish communities (p. 110)

prejudice a dislike of people who are different (p. 41)

quotas limits (p. 44)

racism the belief that one race is superior or inferior to another (p. 41)

Red Scare the height of the anti-immigration hysteria of the 1920s (p. 44)

reform an improvement made in the workplace (p. 84)

refuge a safe place (p. 7)

refugees people who flee from their home country to find safety in another (p. 105)

scrip certificates good toward supplies at company-owned stores (p. 85)

shantytowns crowded areas where large immigrant families lived (p. 70)

sponsors people or organizations who agree to help refugees find jobs and housing (p. 106)

steamship a large steam-powered ship that carried passengers across the ocean (p. 12)

steerage a large open area beneath a ship's deck (p. 13)

strike a refusal to work until employers meet the workers' demands (p. 85)

sweatshops small factories where workers labored from morning until night (p. 82)

task force a group of experts organized to solve a specific problem (p. 81)

tenements crowded buildings with poor sanitation and safety (p. 18)

transcontinental extending across a continent (p. 24)

unauthorized immigrants immigrants who enter the U. S. illegally or who remain after their visas have expired (p. 119)

unions groups of workers who are joined together to protect and improve their working conditions (p. 84)

visas travel permits that allow a person to leave a country (p. 95)

West Indian referring to people from English-speaking islands in the Caribbean (p. 56)

INDEX

ACKNOWLEDGMENTS

Grateful acknowledgment is made to the following publishers, authors, and other copyright holders:

p. 90: "I work, and I work . . ." by Morris Rosenfeld. Used by permission of Smithmark Publishers.

Grateful acknowledgment is made to the following for illustrations, photographs, and reproductions on the pages indicated:

Photo credits: **Cover Photo:** Corbis-Bettmann; **Cover Inset:** UPI/Corbis-Bettmann; **p. 5:** Culver Pictures; **p. 7:** The Granger Collection, New York; **p. 8:** National Archives; **p. 9:** Brown Brothers; **p.10:** Museum of the City of New York; **p. 11:** The Granger Collection, New York; **p. 12:** Davis & Hunt; **p. 13:** Ellis Island Museum; **p. 14:** Corbis-Bettmann; **p. 15:** Statue of Liberty National Monument; **p. 16:** Brown Brothers; **p. 19:** Corbis-Bettman; **p. 20:** Balch Institute for Ethnic Studies Library; **p. 23:** Corbis-Bettmann; **p. 25:** Corbis-Bettmann; **p. 27:** The Granger Collection, New York; **p. 29:** UPI/Corbis-Bettmann; **p. 30:** The Granger Collection; **p. 31:** Brown Brothers; **p. 33:** Corbis-Bettmann; **p. 35:** State Historical Society of Wisconsin; **p. 36:** The Granger Collection, New York; **p. 39:** Collection of David J. and Janice L. Frent; **p. 40:** UPI/Corbis-Bettmann; **p. 43:** Karen Yamauchi for Cherhayeff and Grishar, Inc./Metaform, Inc.; **p. 44:** Karen Yamauchi for Cherhayeff and Grishar, Inc./Metaform, Inc.; **p. 45:** Library of Congress; **p. 47:** Corbis-Bettmann; **p. 48:** UPI/Corbis-Bettmann; **p. 55:** William B. Williams Papers, Manuscript Division, The New York Public Library; **p. 58:** Culver Pictures; **p. 59:** Schomburg Center for Research and Black Culture; **p. 62:** The Research Libraries /The New York Public Library; **p. 65:** Union Pacific Museum Collection; **p. 67:** John F. Kennedy Library; **p. 68:** Immigrant City Archives, Inc.; **p. 70:** Stock Montage, Inc.; **p. 72:** UPI/Corbis-Bettmann; **p. 73:** Corbis-Bettmann; **p. 75:** UPI/Corbis-Bettmann; **p. 79:** Brown Brothers; **p. 80:** Underwood & Underwood/Corbis-Bettmann; **p. 82:** Museum of the City of New York; **p. 83:** Corbis-Bettmann; **p. 85:** United Mine Workers of America; **p. 86:** United Mine Workers of America; **p. 88:** Corbis-Bettmann; **p. 89**: Corbis-Bettmann; **p. 93:** Cuban American National Council, Inc.; **p. 96:** Cuban American National Council, Inc.; **p. 98:** Cuban American National Council, Inc.; **p. 99:** Cuban American National Council, Inc.; **p. 103:** Stock•Boston; **p. 105:** Ted Jackson-The Times-Pilayune; **p. 106:** Ted Jackson-The Times-Pilayune; **p. 108:** Byron Shall/The News; **p. 109:** The Palm Beach Post; **p. 110:** Stan Grossfeld/The Boston Globe; **p. 112:** Sanchez Family; **p. 113:** Sanchez Family; **p. 117:** James Nubile; **p. 118:** Norman McGrath; **p. 120:** James Nubile; **p. 122:** Norman McGrath